PHILOSOPHY OF RELIGION SERIES

Editor's Note

The philosophy of religion is one of several very active branches of philosophy today, and the present series is designed both to consolidate the gains of the past and to direct attention upon the problems of the future. Between them these volumes will cover every aspect of the subject, introducing it to the reader in the state in which it is today, including its open ends and growing points. Thus the series is designed to be used as a comprehensive textbook for students. But it is also offered as a contribution to present-day discussion; and each author will accordingly go beyond the scope of an introduction to formulate his own position in the light of contemporary debates.

JOHN HICK

Philosophy of Religion Series

General Editor: John Hick, H. G. Wood Professor of Theology,
University of Birmingham

Forthcoming titles

Ninian Smart (Lancaster University) The Phenomenon of Religion
William Christian (Yale University)
Oppositions of Religious Doctrines:
An Approach to Claims of Different Religions
M. J. Charlesworth (Melbourne University)
Philosophy of Religion: The Historic Approaches
H. P. Owen (King's College, London) Concepts of Deity
Basil Mitchell (Oriel College, Oxford)
The Language of Religion
Terence Penelhum (Calgary University)
Problems of Religious Knowledge
Nelson Pike (California University)
Religious Experience and Mysticism
Donald Evans (Toronto University) Religion and Morality
Kai Nielsen (New York University)
Contemporary Critiques of Religion
Dennis Nineham (Keble College, Oxford) Faith and History
H. D. Lewis (King's College, London) The Self and Immortality

Arguments for the Existence of God

JOHN HICK

MACMILLAN

First published 1970 by
MACMILLAN AND CO LTD
London and Basingstoke
Associated companies in New York Toronto
Dublin Melbourne Johannesburg and Madras

SBN (boards) 333 05574 8
(paper) 333 11260 1

Printed in Great Britain by
ROBERT MACLEHOSE AND CO LTD
The University Press, Glasgow

Contents

Introduction

In this book we are concerned with philosophical arguments for the existence of God, that is, with theistic arguments which have their place in the history of Western philosophy — these being primarily the cosmological type of reasoning, which goes back to Plato; the teleological, going back to the Stoics; the ontological proof, originated by Anselm; and the family of moral arguments of which Immanuel Kant was the founding father. This restriction to Western thought corresponds to the fact that the notion of proving the reality of the divine by philosophical argument was contributed to the stock of human thought by the ancient Greeks and has borne its fruit, beyond the thought of Plato, Aristotle and the Stoics, within the Western developments of Christianity and Islam.

This means that the arguments with which we are to be concerned are theistic in intent: the God whose existence they seek to prove, or to show to be probable, is the God of ethical monotheism (i.e. of Judaism, Christianity and Islam). We may briefly characterise this conception of the divine as follows. God is the unique infinite personal Spirit who has created out of nothing everything other than himself; he is eternal and uncreated; omnipotent and omniscient; and his attitude to his human creatures is one of grace and love. This is the being whose existence is sought to be established by the arguments we are to examine.

Something should however perhaps be said at this point about the phrase 'God exists', the propriety of which has been challenged on both philosophical and theological grounds. We are not at the moment concerned with the question *whether* God exists, but with the suitability of the locution 'God exists', used either in affirmation or denial. The philosophical objection is that 'x exists' is a logically misleading way of saying something else, namely that the description or definition indicated by the term x is instantiated. Thus the correct question is not whether a being

vii

called God does or does not have the property of existence, but whether the definition of 'God' has or lacks an instance. This well-known Russellian analysis of 'exists' (1) entails that 'God exists' and 'the existence (or the reality) of God' are solecisms. They remain however very convenient solecisms, and they can be rendered harmless by stipulating that 'God exists' is to be construed as shorthand for 'There is an individual, and only one, who is omniscient, omnipotent, etc.' With this understanding it is permissible to retain the traditional phrase even whilst acknowledging its strict impropriety.

The theological objection to speaking of the existence of God is of a quite different kind and is formulated as follows by Paul Tillich: 'Thus the question of the existence of God can be neither asked nor answered. If asked, it is a question about that which by its very nature is above existence, and therefore the answer — whether negative or affirmative — implicitly denies the nature of God. It is as atheistic to affirm the existence of God as it is to deny it. God is being-itself, not *a* being.' (2) This is in effect a theological-semantic recommendation that the term 'existence' be applied only to entities within the created realm, with the result that it becomes improper to assert of a postulated creator of this realm that he *exists*. The recommendation operates as an emphatic rejection of any notion of God as a finite object alongside others in the universe. But we still want to be able to distinguish between there being and there not being an ultimate reality which is not a part of the universe and to which we may properly direct our 'ultimate concern'; and the term 'the existence of God' enables us to do this. Once again, then, it seems on the whole preferable to retain the traditional phrase than to risk concealing important issues by rejecting it.

The traditional theistic arguments are commonly distinguished as being either *a priori* or *a posteriori*. An *a posteriori* argument is one which relies on a premise derived from (hence after or posterior to) experience. Accordingly *a posteriori* arguments for the existence of God infer a deity from evidences within our human experience. An *a priori* argument, on the other hand, operates from a basis which is logically prior to and independent of experience. It rests upon purely logical considerations and (if it succeeds) achieves the kind of certainty exhibited by mathematical truths.

In point of fact only one strictly *a priori* theistic proof has been offered — the ontological argument of Anselm, Descartes and others. This claims on *a priori* grounds that the idea of 'the most perfect and real conceivable being' is the idea of a being which must and therefore does exist; for a Non-existent could never be the most perfect and real conceivable being. This argument has been the subject of a great deal of discussion during the last couple of decades, including the rediscovery of a second form of the proof which some claim to be immune to the traditional criticisms. Chapters 5 and 6 are devoted to the ontological argument in both its forms.

As regards the *a posteriori* theistic proofs it is necessary to distinguish between, on the one hand, those which profess to constitute strict apodictic demonstrations or 'knock-down arguments' and those, on the other hand, which are of the nature of probability arguments, seeking to persuade us that theism is the most reasonable of the available alternatives.

In considering any attempted strict proof of divine existence it is necessary to be clear what 'proof' means in such a context. We must in fact distinguish several different senses of 'prove'. For there are two senses in which we may speak of something being proved in which it is a non-controversial statement that the existence of God can be proved; and these need to be mentioned and set aside in order to isolate the central problem, which concerns a third sense.

The existence of God can undoubtedly be proved if a proof is equated with a formally valid argument. For it is a familiar logical truism that a valid argument can be constructed with *any* proposition as its conclusion. Given any proposition, *q*, it is possible to supply other propositions such that it would be inconsistent to affirm these and to deny *q*. The propositions thus supplied constitute premises from which *q* follows as a conclusion. One can easily construct a proof in this sense for the existence of God. For example: If Birmingham exists, God exists; Birmingham exists; therefore God exists. The argument is formally impeccable — one cannot rationally affirm the premises and deny the conclusion.

However this first sense of 'prove' is referred to here only to be dismissed as an inconvenient and confusing usage. It is much better to follow the more normal practice and to distinguish between an argument being valid and its conclusion being true. The validity of an argument is a purely formal characteristic of the relation between its constituent propositions and does not guarantee the truth of any of them. It guarantees that *if* the premises are true the conclusion is true also; but it cannot guarantee that the premises, and therefore the conclusion, *are* true.

A second sense of 'prove' is that in which a conclusion is said to be proved, not merely if it follows from premises, but if it follows from *true* premises. We may consider this second sense in relation to and in distinction from a third in which these conditions are supplemented by the yet further requirement that the premises are *known* or acknowledged to be true. There might, in sense number two, be all manner of valid arguments in which true premises lead to true conclusions but which do not prove anything to anyone because no one acknowledges their premises as being true. In this sense, all that can be said is that there may be a proof of God's existence *if* God exists but not if he does not! But this is so trivial a point that no one will be concerned to dispute it. It is surely the third sense, in which to prove something means to prove it *to* someone, that is really in question when we ask whether the existence of God can be proved.

The sense of 'prove', then, which most concerns us is that in which we speak of proving a certain conclusion to an individual or a group. Here it is required not only that the conclusion follows from the premises, and not only that the premises from which it follows are true, but also that they are acknowledged to be true by those to whom we are seeking to prove the conclusion. It is at this point that a basic philosophical objection emerges to all strict theistic proofs of the *a posteriori* type — namely that they necessarily beg the question, in that a person who accepts their premises already acknowledges the reality of God. For theistic arguments of this type rely upon some connection between God and the world. In order to provide a basis for a strict proof of God's existence the connection must be such as to warrant the proposition, 'If the world (or some particular aspect of it) exists, God exists'. But clearly anyone who accepts this premise already either acknowledges the existence of God or else is unable to reason at all. And it is idle to offer a demonstration to one who does not need it or is incapable of using it. Those, on the other hand, who do not accept the premise will never be led by this route to affirm the reality of God.

But might one not become converted to this premise by considering the implications of an additional premise — that the world must be ultimately explicable by reference to some reality beyond itself, and is not a sheer inexplicable 'brute fact' that can only be accepted as such? As Father Copleston says in the course of his debate with Bertrand Russell, 'my point is that what we call the world is intrinsically unintelligible, apart from the existence of God'. (3) The first cause argument and the argument from contingency both employ this principle either explicitly or implicitly. Their logical form is that of a dilemma: either there is a God or the world is ultimately unintelligible. The one argument urges that either there is an endless and therefore meaningless regress of causes or else the causal series must finally be anchored in an uncaused first cause, which is God. The other argument claims that each item in nature points beyond itself for its sufficient explanation, and urges that either the regress of explanations runs out to infinity, with the result that nothing is ever finally explained, or else it must terminate in a self-existent being which neither needs nor is capable of further explanation; and this is God. Clearly the force of these arguments depends upon the decisive ruling out of one alternative, namely that the world is ultimately inexplicable, so that we shall be driven by force of logic to the other conclusion, that God exists. But the difficulty of finding an agreed premise arises again at this point. For it is precisely this excluding of the non-theistic alternative that apparently is not and cannot be accomplished by logical considerations alone. It rests upon a fundamental act of faith, faith in the ultimate 'rationality' of existence; and this is part of the larger faith which the atheist refuses. He believes on the contrary that the universe is devoid of ultimate meaning or purpose and that the question as to why there is anything at all has no meaning and therefore no answer. This cosmo-logical type of reasoning will be examined more fully in Chapter 3.

Whilst the first cause argument and the argument from the contingency of the world profess to be strictly demon-strative, the other *a posteriori* arguments, particularly the design and moral arguments, attempt to establish a high probability rather than a logical certainty. They direct attention to some aspect of the world or of human experience — for example, the order and beauty of nature and its apparently purposive character, or man's ethical experience and appreciation of values — and conclude that this is most adequately explained by postulating a divine creator or a transcendent ground of value. It is not claimed that the intellectual move from these starting-points to God proceeds on the ironclad rails of logical entailment. There can be no strict deduction of an infinite deity from the character of finite things. Rather these function as significant signs and clues, pointing with varying degrees of particularity and force to the reality of God. Formulated as arguments directed to the non-believer, such inferences accordingly centre upon the notion of probability. Their general form is: in view of this or that characteristic of the world it is more probable that there is a God than that there is not. The design argument — since the eighteenth century the one to have made the widest appeal — and the notion of probability in relation to theistic arguments are discussed in Chapters 1 and 2.

The moral argument, as it has generally been formulated, fails to impress the atheist because it clashes *ab initio* with the naturalistic type of ethical theory which he holds. The argument is thus foiled at the outset by the difficulty of finding an agreed premise. But in Chapter 4 I suggest that it is possible to start from a naturalistic ethical theory and to show that some of the acts which an atheist most highly respects and praises are incapable of rational justification on the basis of his own theory — so that the naturalistic picture of man and his place in the universe is insufficient. This does not prove the existence of God; but by raising a question to which God could be the answer it shows such an existence to be possible.

And this, I suggest, is what all of the traditional theistic arguments do. They establish the *possibility* of God by pointing to aspects of human experience which pose problems in reflecting upon which we find ourselves faced with the alternatives of accepting sheer formless and meaningless mystery or the worship-eliciting mystery of God. We may choose the former; but the latter always remains as an open possibility. The way in which the different theistic arguments fail to establish the existence of God but succeed in establishing the possibility of God will be the theme of the succeeding chapters.

At various times in the past these traditional arguments have been regarded as being of major religious importance; for they answered the question, Is it reasonable to believe in God? But the prevailing contemporary theological view of them (of which the opinion I have expressed above is a variant) is not only that they do not prove the existence of God but also that it was a mistake to think that any such proof could ever be constructed. In the last chapter I therefore enter into the contemporary discussion concerning the rationality of belief in the reality of an unproved God.

But even if the theistic arguments are not religiously important they remain philosophically important. They are classic pieces of reasoning, inextricably intertwined with the rest of the history of Western philosophy. Anyone who has grappled with the concepts of necessity, existence, perfection and deity involved in the ontological argument; with the notions of causality and explanation involved in the cosmological argument; with the ideas of order and purpose which occur in the teleological argument; and with the question of the metaphysical implications of ethics raised by the moral arguments, has already received a philosophical education.

A number of friends have read and criticised one or other or several of the following chapters, and I have as a result been able to make the book much less inadequate that it would otherwise have been.

The various basic writings, from Plato to the present day, which are discussed here are collected together in my book of readings 'The Existence of God' (New York: Macmillan, and London: Collier-Macmillan, 1964), which thus forms a companion volume to the present work. (4)

1 The Design Argument

(a) Introductory

The teleological or design argument, proceeding from the world as exhibiting intelligible order to a divine intelligence as the source of that order, is very ancient. (1) It perhaps has its earliest roots in the thought of Plato, who argued that the physical universe is unintelligible apart from mind, which moves and orders it. (2) However that idea has developed more readily, from the point of view of our medieval and modern distinctions, into the 'cosmological' than into the 'teleological' proof. The classic exposition in the ancient world of a form of reasoning which is continuous with what we today call the design argument comes from the Stoic philosopher Lucilius Balbus (reported in Cicero's 'De Natura Deorum'), who describes the strongest ground of theistic belief as one which 'is drawn from the regularity of the motion and revolution of the heavens, the distinctness, variety, beauty, and order of the sun, moon, and all the stars, the appearance only of which is sufficient to convince us they are not the effects of chance'. (3)

After its first appearance in ancient Greece the argument had its second life in medieval Europe. It occurs as the fifth of Aquinas's 'Five Ways' and was employed by a number of other theologians in the latter Middle Ages. But its greatest flourishing was in the seventeenth and eighteenth centuries when the development of the descriptive sciences, particularly zoology, botany, astronomy and anatomy enabled the teleologist to illustrate his case with hundreds of examples of adaptation and therefore, he assumed, of design in nature. Much of the literature developing this theme was produced in England, two notable series of volumes propagating the gospel of an evident divine arrangement of the natural world being the 'Boyle Lectures' (4) and the 'Bridgewater Treatises on the Power, Wisdom and Goodness of God as Manifest in the Creation' (8 vols, London, 1833-40). Indeed the design

1

argument, as a feature of the thought-world of 'eighteenth-century optimism', moved through christian apologetics and philosophical preaching in this country with an impetus which was to carry it on into the Victorian age to do battle with Darwinism.

It was likewise in the eighteenth century that the design argument met its most formidable philosophical critic, David Hume. However, the argument went on being reformulated long after Hume, one of the most widely used versions coming in William Paley's 'Natural Theology, or Evidences of the Existence and Attributes of the Deity, collected from the Appearances of Nature', published in 1802. This was a standard work of christian apologetics in the English-speaking world throughout the nineteenth century, and as recently as the 1950s one could meet elderly ministers, educated towards the end of last century, who had been brought up on Paley. Paley's arguments are now defunct; but the design argument itself has not died with the passing years. It was revived in the last generation by two British philosophers, F. R. Tennant (5) and A. E. Taylor (6), and by the French physicist Pierre Lecomte du Noüy; (7) and within the last few years one aspect of it has been interestingly reformulated by the American philosopher Richard Taylor. (8)

It is impossible in the space available to describe and discuss every historically important formulation of the argument; and indeed in view of the largely repetitive character of the relevant literature this would prove neither interesting nor useful. I shall instead present the eighteenth-century version of the argument, Hume's critique and the way in which Darwin's work has reinforced some of Hume's arguments; and then the much more recent versions offered by Tennant, du Noüy and Richard Taylor.

(b) The eighteenth-century design argument

For the eighteenth-century argument we can hardly do better than begin with Paley's famous version of the analogy of the watch. When the eighteenth-century apologists compared the workings of the solar system and of terrestrial nature with that of a machine, the example of mechanical design that

2

most readily came to mind was the clock which stood on the mantlepiece in every reader's drawing-room — for the readers of popular philosophy and theology were of course the gentry, from the sale of whose libraries by their descendants we in these latter days have acquired our leather-bound copies of Ray and Derham and Paley and the rest.

The passage introducing 'Paley's Watch' occurs at the beginning of his *Natural Theology*:

> In crossing a heath, suppose I pitched my foot against a *stone*, and were asked how the stone came to be there; I might possibly answer, that, for anything I knew to the contrary, it had lain there for ever: nor would it perhaps be very easy to show the absurdity of this answer. But suppose I had found a *watch* upon the ground and it should be inquired how the watch happened to be in that place; I should hardly think of the answer which I had before given, that, for anything I knew, the watch might have been always there. Yet why should not this answer serve for the watch as well as for the stone? Why is it not as admissable in the second case, as in the first? For this reason, and for no other, viz. that, when we come to inspect the watch, we perceive (what we could not discover in the stone) that its several parts are framed and put together for a purpose, e.g. that they are so formed and adjusted as to produce motion, and that motion so regulated as to point out the hour of the day; that, if the different parts had been differently shaped from what they are, or placed after any other manner, or in any other order, than that in which they are placed, either no motion at all would have been carried on in the machine, or none which would have answered the use that is now served by it. (9)

Paley then develops particular aspects of his analogy. I am referring here to the first four of his eight points in chapter 1 (the last four adding nothing new of any significance), together with the argument in chapter 2. First, it does not weaken our inference from watch to watchmaker if we have never seen a watch being made: the object itself convinces us that it is a product of intelligence. Nor, second, does it

3

materially weaken this inference if the watch does not appear to work perfectly: we can still appreciate that it must have come about by design instead of being produced by the random operation of such natural forces as wind and rain. Nor again, third, would it cast doubt upon the inference if there should be parts of the watch whose function we cannot discover, or even parts which so far as we can tell have no function: despite this the watch could not have come about without a watchmaker. Fourth — and here Paley may have had in mind an argument derived from Hume's *Dialogues*, published twenty-three years earlier (10) — no one in his senses could 'think the existence of the watch, with its various machinery, accounted for, by being told it was one out of possible combinations of material forms; that whatever he had found in the place where he found the watch, must have contained some internal configuration or other; and that this configuration might be the structure now exhibited, viz. of the works of a watch, as well as a different structure'. (11) Fifth — and this again may refer to an argument of Hume's — no one would be satisfied 'to be answered, that there existed in things a principle of order, which had disposed the parts of the watch into their present form and situation. He never knew a watch made by the principle of order; nor can he even form to himself an idea of what is meant by a principle of order, distinct from the intelligence of the watch-maker.' (12) And sixth, if we found that the watch included a mechanism for manufacturing further watches, so that the watch we had found had probably itself been made by a previous watch, and so on back in time, this would not counter our inference to an original watchmaker: on the contrary it would only increase our admiration for the genius of the designer of such complex self-producing machines.

This being so, Paley is now able to apply his analogy directly to the world, claiming that 'every indication of contrivance, every manifestation of design, which existed in the watch, exists in the works of nature; with the difference, on the side of nature, of being greater and more, and that in a degree which exceeds all computation. I mean, that the contrivances of nature surpass the contrivances of art, in the complexity, subtility, and curiosity of the mechanism; and

4

still more, if possible, do they go beyond them in number and variety; yet, in a multitude of cases, are not less evidently mechanical, not less evidently contrivances, not less evidently accommodated to their end, or suited to their office, than are the most perfect productions of human ingenuity.' (13)

In the course of his book Paley discusses in detail many instances of the suitablility of the bodily structure of animals, birds and fishes to the conditions of their life on the earth, in the air, or in the sea. For example, 'there is precisely the same proof that the eye was made for vision, as there is that the telescope was made for assisting it.' (14)

And if Paley had lived more recently he would doubtless have compared the eye, to even greater effect, with a cine camera taking a colour film. There are similar arrangements of adjustable lenses and light- and colour-sensitive surfaces, with a bonus in the case of the eye of an automatic mechanism for washing the lense.

But instead of staying with Paley, let us further sample the flavour of the eighteenth-century design argument by opening William Derham's works. His *Physico-Theology: or, A Demonstration of the Being and Attributes of God, from his Works of Creation*, first published in 1713 and containing the Boyle Lectures for 1711 and 1712, went through many editions during the following decades. After citing dozens of examples of adaptation in animal life Derham sums up:

And upon the whole matter, what less can be concluded, than that there is a Being infinitely wise, potent, and kind, who is able to contrive and make this glorious scene of things, which I have thus given only a glance of? For what less than infinite, could stock so vast a globe with such a noble set of animals? All so contrived, as to minister to one another's help some way or other, and most of them servicable to man peculiarly, the top of this lower world, and who was made, as it were, on purpose to observe and survey, and set forth the glory of the infinite Creator, manifested in his works! Who? What, but the great God, could so admirably provide for the whole animal world, everything servicable to it, or that can be wished for, either to conserve its species, or to minister to the being or well-being of individuals! Particularly, who could feed so

5

spacious a world, who could please so large a number of palates, or suit so many palates to so great a variety of food, but the infinite Conservator of the world! And who but the same great He, could provide such commodious clothing for every animal; such proper houses, nests, and habitations; such suitable armature and weapons; such subtilty, artifice, and sagacity, as every creature is more or less armed and furnished with, to fence off the injuries of the weather, to rescue itself from dangers, to preserve itself from the annoyances of its enemies; and, in a word, to conserve itself, and its species! What but an infinite superintending Power could so equally balance the several species of animals, and conserve the numbers of the individuals of every species so even, as not to over or under-people the terraqueous globe! (15)

The next year, in 1714, Derham published a companion volume, his *Astro-Theology: or, A Demonstration of the Being and Attributes of God, from a Survey of the Heavens*, from which I shall quote only one characteristic piece of reasoning:

When we see divers pieces of curious device and workmanship to bear the same marks of art, to have the same masterly strokes of painting, clockwork, architecture, etc. we conclude with great reason such pieces were made by the same skilful hand. So when we see the same commodious spherical figure to be imparted to the earth, and all the heavenly bodies, we have as good reason to conclude them to be pieces of the same hand, contrivances and works of the same skilful architect. For if the universe had been a work of chance, all the several globes would have been of several forms, one of this, another of a quite different figure: one square, another multangular, another long, and another of another shape. . . . (16)

I shall only add to this a much more recent argument, of which Derham would certainly have approved, found in a book called 'Footprints of God'. The author refers to the ozone layer in the atmosphere which filters out enough of the burning ultra-violet rays of the sun to make life as we

6

know it possible on the surface of the earth. 'The Ozone gas layer is a mighty proof of the Creator's forethought. Could anyone possibly attribute this device to a chance evolutionary process? A wall which prevents death to every living thing, just the right thickness, and exactly the correct defense, gives every evidence of plan.' (17)

(c) Hume's critique

When David Hume (1711-76), with the possible exception of Duns Scotus Scotland's greatest philosopher, and a major figure in the history of British empiricism, wrote a critique of contemporary natural theology it was inevitable that his attack should centre upon the design argument. In order to see why his book is in the form of a dialogue — modelled upon Cicero's 'De Natura Deorum' — we have to take note of Hume's personal and social situation. The design argument was deeply entrenched in the minds of his contemporaries, and it would be hard to reconcile a direct rejection of it with the tacit intellectual 'concordat' which governed Hume's friendly relations with many of the leading moderate churchmen of his day. For although well known as 'Hume the Sceptic', he was a respected member of a distinguished Edinburgh circle in one of that city's greatest periods. The Athens of the North provided as familiar friends of Hume's Adam Smith, the economist; Hugh Blair, leading liberal churchman; William Robertson, Principal of the University; Lord Kames and Lord Elibank, judges; Allan Ramsay, the portrait painter; and a number of other influential men within whose society Hume played a leading part. In these circles Hume was regarded as being, like all decent men, a believer in God — though in the remote deity of philosophy rather than the God of popular religion. However the argument developed in the 'Dialogues' puts this theistic or deistic assumption under considerable strain. Not only is the great eighteenth-century bulwark of belief in God, the design argument, subjected to powerful criticism, but in the second, fourth and twelfth dialogues (further sharpened in this direction in Hume's final revision) (18) it is suggested that the concept of God must, in philosophic minds, be so

7

qualified that theism and atheism become in the end merely alternative ways of describing the same facts. How was Hume to present such unpalatable views without isolating himself from the society of his friends and acquaintances? For although in the end Hume did not himself publish the 'Dialogues', but left the manuscript to be printed after his death by his nephew, he had completed it (though making some additions during the months before his death) at least fifteen years earlier, and much of it twenty-five years earlier; and he had originally intended to publish it then, but was dissuaded by his friends. Intending, then, to make his criticisms of natural theology public, he preferred not to utter them directly in his own voice but to allow them to emerge by their own force through a dialogue in which all the major contemporary points of view were represented. Indeed ostensibly it is not the sceptic, Philo, but the upholder of the design argument, Cleanthes, (19) with whom the reporter of the discussion expresses his agreement in the last paragraph. And this device has succeeded in misleading many readers, including some philosophical commentators. But it seems to me that the evidence of Hume's other writings is decisively in favour of the view argued by Kemp Smith in his critical edition of the 'Dialogues' that 'Philo, from start to finish, represents Hume, and that Cleanthes can be regarded as Hume's mouthpiece only in those passages in which he is explicitly agreeing with Philo, or in those other passages in which, while refuting Demea, he is being used to prepare the way for one or other of Philo's independent conclusions'. (20) Adopting this interpretation I shall not scruple to speak of Hume as making this or that point when, within the dialogue, it is Philo who makes it.

Hume, then, develops a number of telling counter-arguments, which I shall here conflate into five, against the inference from the apparently designed character of the world to a divine designer.

The first is the weakness of the analogy between the world and a human artefact, such as a house, a clock, a ship, a knitting-loom or a city. If the world were sufficiently like a known product of human design we should be entitled to infer that, like it, the world is a product of purposive activity. 'But surely you will not affirm, that the universe bears such a

8

resemblance to a house, that we can with the same certainty infer a similar cause, or that the analogy is here entire and perfect. The dissimilitude is so striking, that the utmost you can here pretend to is a guess, a conjecture, a presumption concerning a similar cause.' (21) (Indeed if the world were sufficiently house-like there would be no need to build houses! We only make houses — or clocks — because the world is *not* really very like one.) Further emphasising the tenuousness of the world—artefact analogy, Hume later points out that one could equally well make a case for regarding the world, not as a vast machine, but as a vast crustacean-like organism, or again as a vast floating vegetable. The point he is making is that all such comparisons, including the one relied upon in the design argument, are alike weak and unverifiable: 'we have no *data* to establish any system of cosmogony. Our experience, so imperfect in itself, and so limited both in extent and duration, can afford us no probable conjecture concerning the whole of things. But if we must needs fix on some hypothesis; by what rule, pray, ought we to determine our choice? Is there any other rule than the greater similarity of the objects compared? And does not a plant or an animal, which springs from vegetation or generation, bear a stronger resemblance to the world, than does any artificial machine, which arises from reason and design?' (22)

Second, the design argument explains the order found in nature by tracing its cause to a prior order existing in the mind of the creator. This reasoning assumes that a mental order — the order in the divine mind — is not in need of explanation whereas a physical order is. But, Hume asks:

Allowing that we were to take the *operations* of one part of nature upon another for the foundation of our judgement concerning the *origin* of the whole (which can never be admitted); yet why select so minute, so weak, so bounded a principle [in the eighteenth-century sense of 'cause'] as the reason and design of animals is found to be upon this planet? What peculiar privilege has this little agitation of the brain which we call thought, that we must thus make it the model of the whole universe? Our

9

partiality in our own favour does indeed present it on all occasions: But sound philosophy ought carefully to guard against so natural an illusion. (23)

By what right, then, would we be satisfied by finding the order of the material world prefigured in a prior world of ideas? 'Have we not the same reason to trace that ideal world into another ideal world, or new intelligent principle? But if we stop, and go no farther; why go so far? Why not stop at the material world?' (24)

Third, it is not enough for the protagonist of the design argument simply to point, as did the eighteenth-century apologists, to the ordered state of the universe. For any universe, in order to exist at all, must be a sufficiently coherent and stable complex of elements; and any such system is capable of being regarded as the expression of deliberate design. Any world will *look* designed, however it has come into existence. 'It is in vain, therefore, to insist upon the uses of the parts in animals or vegetables, and their curious adjustment to each other. I would fain known how an animal could subsist, unless its parts were so adjusted?' (25) In other words, it is not sufficient, as warrant for an inference from the world to God, to show that the world is an orderly and self-sustaining system. It must also be shown that this order could not have come about except by divine activity. But this is just what cannot be done; for it is in principle possible to give a speculative account of the ordered state of the universe on purely naturalistic principles. Suppose — as in what Hume calls the Epicurean hypothesis — that the universe consists of a finite number of atoms moving about at random. If there is any possible combination of these atoms that constitutes a self-maintaining order it is virtually inevitable that in infinite time they will sooner or later fall into this combination. Perhaps, then, we are in such a universe and in such a state of temporary or long-lived order which has arisen by chance out of a situation of randomness.

Since Hume's day the hypothesis of a self-regulating development of order has been strongly confirmed in the biological sphere. For some time before the publication of Charles Darwin's epoch-making 'Origin of Species' in 1859 a number of biologists had surmised that the various species inhabiting the globe were descended from one or only a few original kinds of simpler organism. But until Darwin showed the detailed stages of this development the theory of evolution remained speculative. Darwin turned the speculation into a concrete and convincing model of the history of life on our planet. He showed that the mechanism of evolution was a process of natural selection operating on the stream of descent by inheritance with variations provided by mutations. During the last forty or so years this picture has been further amplified by new discoveries in genetics. To quote Julian Huxley, the evolutionary process 'results immediately and automatically from the basic property of living matter — that of self-copying, but with occasional errors. Self-copying leads to multiplication and competition; the errors in self-copying are what we call mutations, and mutations will inevitably confer different degrees of biological advantage or disadvantage on their possessors. The consequence will be differential reproduction down the generations — in other words, natural selection.' (26) And 'selective advantages so small as to be undetectable in any one generation, are capable, when operating on the scale of geological time, of producing all the observed phenomena of biological evolution.' (27) Thus new species have gradually evolved and life has grown from its simplest forms to its present multiplicity of kinds, including man.

In its relation to the design argument this evolutionary picture can be seen as spelling out Hume's 'Epicurean hypothesis' in one very important sphere — that of the fittedness of the different parts of a living organism to minister to the organism's survival, and the adaptation of organisms to the environment. Thus the Darwinian theory of the origin of species by means of natural selection offers a causal explanation of those features of animate life which had been appealed to by the pre-Darwinian teleologists as evidence of a divine designer.

Fourth, the inference to God from the appearances of nature can never entitle us to affirm the infinite and perfect creator depicted in Christian theology. For a finite and imperfect world, as effect, cannot entail an infinite and perfect creator as its cause. We are only authorised, at best,

11

to postulate as much in the divine cause as is required to account for the observed effect. In a figure which Hume used in the 'Enquiries' as well as the 'Dialogues', if one end of a pair of scales is visible and the other concealed and the visible end, containing ten ounces, is weighed down we can infer that the other, which outweighs it, contains more than ten ounces; but we cannot infer that it contains a hundred ounces, and still less that it contains an infinitely heavy weight. (28)

So the God of the design argument must not be affirmed to be infinite in goodness, power, wisdom or skill:

> If we survey a ship, what an exalted idea must we form of the ingenuity of the carpenter, who framed so complicated, useful, and beautiful a machine? And what surprise must we entertain, when we find him a stupid mechanic, who imitated others, and copied an art, which, through a long succession of ages, after multiplied trials, mistakes, corrections, deliberations, and controversies, had been gradually improving? Many worlds might have been botched and bungled, throughout an eternity, ere this system was struck out: Much labour lost: Many fruitless trials made: And a slow, but continued improvement carried on during infinite ages in the art of world-making. (29)

Nor, again, may we assume that the divine source of the world is unitary: 'A great number of men join in building a house or ship, in rearing a city, in framing a commonwealth: Why may not several Deities combine in contriving and framing a world? This is only so much greater similarity to human affairs.' (30) Why not, then, troops of gods and godesses, as in the ancient Greek pantheon? And Hume (in the person of Philo) concludes:

> In a word, Cleanthes, a man, who follows your hypothesis, is able, perhaps, to assert, or conjecture, that the universe, sometime, arose from something like design: But beyond that position he cannot ascertain one single circumstance, and is left afterwards to fix every point of his theology, by the utmost licence of fancy and hypothesis. This world, for aught he knows, is very faulty and imperfect,

12

compared to a superior standard; and was only the first rude essay of some infant Deity, who afterwards abandoned it, ashamed of his lame performance; it is the work only of some dependent, inferior Deity; and is the object of derision to his superiors: it is the production of old age and dotage in some superannuated Deity; and ever since his death, has run on at adventures, from the first impulse and active force, which it received from him. (31)

A fifth acute point of Hume's questions the use of the notion of probability in relation to the existence of God, in view of the fact that the universe is unique:

When two *species* of objects have always been observed to be conjoined together, I can *infer*, by custom, the existence of one wherever I *see* the existence of the other: And this I call an argument from experience. But how this argument can have place, where the objects, as in the present case, are single, individual, without parallel, or specific resemblance, may be difficult to explain. And will any man tell me with a serious countenance, that an orderly universe must arise from some thought and art, like the human; because we have experience of it? To ascertain this reasoning, it were requisite, that we had experience of the origin of worlds. (32)

Hume does not elaborate this argument against probability judgements concerning the universe. But it is extremely important, striking as it does at the root of both the design argument and the other members of the family of probability arguments for God. One might however take Hume's point as being directed, not against probability judgements in the strict sense but more broadly against analogical reasoning concerning the origin of the universe. Understood in this way, Hume's objection would fail. For the fact that the universe is unique does not rule out the possibility of similarities between it and some of its parts, and therefore between its cause and the cause of those parts. As Alvin Plantinga points out in the course of a valuable discussion of this passage of Hume's, 'The mere fact that a thing is unique does not of course entail that it has no property in common

13

with anything else.' (33) If, for example, the universe could be shown to be sufficiently like something — say, a clock — which is known to be a product of purposive intelligence, there would be a valid analogical inference to the production of the universe itself by a purposive intelligence. But of course this is just what Hume denies in his main attack on the design argument (see pp. 8-9 above). I therefore think it is proper to understand Hume's reference to the uniqueness of the universe as related to probability judgements rather than as related to analogical reasoning in general. Seeing it in this light I shall devote part of the next chapter to it (see section *(b)*) and will therefore not pursue the matter further at this point.

It is not I think necessary to say anything about Immanuel Kant's influential criticism, in the 'Critique of Pure Reason' (chapter III of the Transcendental Dialectic), of what he called the physico-theological proof, for he did not add any significant new arguments to those which he had encountered in Hume's 'Dialogues', read by him in the manuscript of J. G. Hamann's German translation. (34)

(d) Modern restatements: (1) Lecomte du Noüy

Although chronologically the contribution of the French physicist Pierre Lecomte du Noüy comes after that of F. R. Tennant, yet logically it occupies an intermediate point between the positions of Paley and Tennant; and I therefore propose to discuss du Noüy first.

He argued that the improbability of the chance formation of the basic chemical constituents of living organisms is so great that 'it is *totally impossible* to account scientifically for all phenomena pertaining to Life, its development and progressive evolution.' (35) From this du Noüy concludes that we must postulate the intervention of a parascientific 'anti-chance' factor in the evolution of the universe; and 'For a man of science there is no difference between the meaning of the words "anti-chance" and "God".' (36) In short, 'our entire organised, living universe becomes incomprehensible without the hypothesis of God.' (37)

In seeking to establish this conclusion du Noüy discusses

14

the coming to be of a molecule of protein, this being a basic constituent of living substances. A molecule of protein is itself a fairly complex formation, although it is only one of the many and various ingredients of organic life. Du Noüy tries to calculate the probability of the appearance by chance alone of a single molecule of protein. For the purposes of the calculation he is supposing this molecule to contain only 2,000 atoms (this being true of the simplest proteins) and these atoms to be of only two different kinds (whereas in reality they are of at least four), ordered in a very simple pattern with dissymmetry of 0·9. These are deliberately simplifying assumptions which have the effect of over- rather than underestimating the probability under investigation. Du Noüy reports that according to the calculation of Charles-Eugène Guye the probability of such a molecule coming about by chance would be

$$2 \cdot 02 \times 10^{-321} \text{ or } 2 \cdot 02 \times \frac{1}{10^{321}}$$

He continues:

The volume of substance necessary for such a probability to take place is beyond all imagination. It would be that of a sphere with a radius so great that light would take 10^{82} years to cover this distance. The volume is incomparably greater than that of the whole universe including the farthest galaxies, whose light takes only 2×10^6 (two million) years to reach us. In brief, we would have to imagine a volume more than one sextillion, sextillion, sextillion times greater than the Einsteinian universe (Charles-Eugène Guye).

The probability for a *single* molecule of high dissymmetry to be formed by the action of chance and normal thermic agitation remains practically nil. Indeed, if we suppose 500 trillion shakings per second (5×10^{14}), which corresponds to the order of magnitude of light frequencies (wave lengths comprised between 0·4 and 0·8 microns), we find that the time needed to form, on an average, one such molecule (degree of dissymmetry 0·9) in a material volume equal to that of our terrestrial globe is about 10^{242} billions of years (1 followed by 243 zeros).

15

But we must not forget that the earth has only existed for two billion years and that life appeared about one billion years ago, as soon as the earth had cooled $(1 \times 10^9$ years).

We thus find ourselves in the case of the player who does not have at his disposal the time necessary to throw his die often enough to have one single chance of obtaining his series, but instead of a period three or four hundred times too short, we are faced with an interval which is more than 10^{243} times too short. . . .

Life itself is not even in question but merely one of the substances which constitute living beings. Now, one molecule is of no use. Hundreds of millions of *identical* ones are necessary. We would need much greater figures to 'explain' the appearance of a series of similar molecules, the improbability increasing considerably as we have seen, for each new molecule (compound probability), and for each series of identical throws. If the probability of appearance of a living cell could be expressed mathematically the preceeding figures would seem negligible. . . .

Events which, even when we admit very numerous experiments, reactions, or shakings per second, *need an infinitely longer time than the estimated duration of the earth in order to have one chance, on an average, to manifest themselves can, it would seem, be considered as impossible in the human sense.* (38)

From this du Noüy draws his conclusion that we cannot rationally account for the phenomenon of life without postulating the anti-chance factor which he equates with God.

The fallacy within this argument has been well exposed by Wallace I. Matson. (39) The improbability of which du Noüy speaks is that of a protein molecule suddenly being formed by chance out of a random distribution of atoms. There is indeed an astronomical order of probability against the instantaneous collection and combination with the appropriate internal arrangements of the upwards of two thousand atoms constituting a protein molecule. But this is not what natural science supposes to have happened. 'The evolutionary concept is that just as man is the last stage reached to date of an immensely slow and complicated

16

process of successive modifications in less complex creatures, so also the protein molecule itself is the resultant of a very large number of successive stages of synthesis, beginning with quite simple compounds.' (40) Thus the probability of protein coming into existence in nature is not the probability (or improbability) defined by du Noüy's calculation, but 'the product of the probabilities of conditions permitting the steps of the synthesis to be realised in succession'. (41) And, as Matson further points out, we do not have (nor is it likely that we ever shall have) sufficient comparative information about the conditions at different stages in the history of our own planet and of other comparable planets to be able to conclude anything about the frequency, and hence the probability, with which the various stages in the formation of protein occur in the relevant situations.

Although du Noüy does not in his book refer to this, a considerable amount of chemical and biochemical research has been directed upon the question of the original formation both of proteins and of the other basic constituent of evolving life, nucleic acid. (42) The outcome to date of this still continuing work seems to be that it is entirely credible that in the 'primeval soup' polymers of amino-acids constituting primitive proteins were formed automatically by 'the experimentally demonstrated capacity of molecules to order themselves'. (43)

In short, then, du Noüy's argument is altogether lacking in cogency.

2 Teleology and Probability

(a) Modern restatements of the design argument:
(2) F. R. Tennant

F. R. Tennant (1866-1957), who was active as a writer throughout the first half of the century, teaching for many years at Cambridge University, produced in his two-volume 'Philosophical Theology' (Cambridge University Press, 1928 and 1930, reprinted 1968) what many have regarded as the ablest presentation of a natural theology from within our science-oriented Western culture. Tennant regarded the nineteenth-century approach to God through religious experience as a mistake and continued the work of the seventeenth- and eighteenth-century deists, who believed that the reality of God could be established by philosophical reasoning from the evidences of nature.

However he rejected the rationalist ideal of a strict demonstrative proof, believing that alike in science, in ordinary life and in religion we live and can only live by venturing upon probabilities. Accordingly he sought to establish the 'theistic hypothesis' as the most probable explanation of the world, man himself with his distinctive powers and experiences being seen as part of the world that is to be explained.

But although Tennant's 'empirical approach to theism' is thus in principle continuous with that of the early Boyle Lecturers, or of Paley or the authors of the 'Bridgewater Treatises', Tennant wrote after the delayed impact of Hume's 'Dialogues' had been felt and after Darwin's evolutionary conception had become generally accepted. (1) Accordingly his argument is more complex and more widely based than those of the earlier design apologists. Tennant describes his programme of 'cosmic teleology' as follows:

The forcibleness of Nature's suggestion that she is the outcome of intelligent design lies not in particular cases of adaptedness in the world, nor even in the multiplicity of

18

them. It is conceivable that every such instance may individually admit of explanation other than in terms of cosmic or 'external' teleology. And if it also admits of teleological interpretation, that fact will not of itself constitute a rigorous certification of external design. The forcibleness of the world's appeal consists rather in the conspiration of innumerable causes to produce, by their united and reciprocal action, and to maintain, a general order of Nature. Narrower kinds of teleological argument based on surveys of restricted spheres of fact, are much more precarious than that for which the name of 'the wider teleology' may be appropriated in that the comprehensive design-argument is the outcome of synopsis or conspection of the knowable world. (2)

Tennant's detailed argument has five strands, and the strength he claims for it is that of all these woven together.

First, 'the mutual adaptation of thought and things, Nature and Knowledge'. (3) There are two aspects of this: 'the primary epistemological contribution to teleological reasoning consists in the fact that the world is more or less intelligible, in that it happens to be more or less of a cosmos, when conceivably it might have been a self-subsistent and determinate "chaos" in which similar events never occurred, none recurred, universals had no place, relations no fixity, things no nexus of determination and "real" categories no foothold.' (4) And secondly, 'It is in that Nature evokes thought of richer kind than is involved in scientific knowledge, and responds to thinking such as is neither logically necessary nor biologically needful, thus suggesting a Beyond, that considerations as to the relation between thought and things assume their chief significance for the teleologist.' (5)

Second, the most significant aspect of the adaptation of organisms to their environment is not the mechanism by which this has come about — as to this Tennant is prepared to accept the kind of description offered by Darwinism — but 'the progressiveness of the evolutionary process... as a whole'. (6) For 'The discovery of organic evolution has caused the teleologist to shift his ground from special design in the products to directivity in the process, and plan in the primary collocations.' (7) After all, 'The survival of the fittest presupposes the arrival of the fit.' (8) Tennant is suggesting that whilst the mechanism whereby the species are under continual pressure to become better adapted to their environment can indeed be described without reference to a Designer, nevertheless the existence of the whole process as a successful going-concern remains unexplained and can best be accounted for by the theistic hypothesis.

Third, there is the fitness of the physical world to produce and sustain life. 'The fitness of our world to be the home of living beings depends upon certain primary conditions, astronomical, thermal, chemical, etc., and on the coincidence of qualities apparently not causally connected with one another, the number of which would doubtless surprise anyone wholly unlearned in the sciences; and these primary conditions, in their turn, involve many of secondary order. Unique assemblages of unique properties on so vast a scale being thus essential to the maintenance of life, their forthcomingness makes the inorganic world seem in some respects comparable with an organism. It is suggestive of a formative principle.' (9) It is no doubt logically possible that the complex, life-producing physical order came about as a result of the chance movements of molecules, as in Hume's 'Epicurean hypothesis'; but this is enormously improbable. 'Presumably the world is comparable with a single throw of dice. And common sense is not foolish in suspecting the dice to have been loaded.' (10)

Fourth, 'Besides possessing a structure that happens to render it habitable by living creatures and intelligible to some of them, the world is a bearer of values, thus evincing affinity with beings such as can appreciate as well as understand.' (11) Tennant is referring here especially to aesthetic values. Nature is everywhere producing beauty. And 'Nature's beauty is of a piece with the world's intelligibility and with its being a theatre for moral life; and thus far the case for theism is strengthened by aesthetic considerations.' (12)

Fifth, there is the significance of man's moral nature, as an aspect of the universe that is to be explained. For to insist that man is part of nature is by implication to require that any explanation of nature shall also be adequate to cover man. The natural world is so structured as to have produced

20

rational and ethical life; and this is something that must be accounted for in any reasonable explanation of the universe. 'Nature, then, has produced moral beings, is instrumental to moral life and therefore amenable to "instrumental" moral valuation, and is relatively modifiable by operative moral ideas — or, rather, by moral agents pursuing ideals. Nature and moral man are not at strife, but are organically one. The whole process of Nature is capable of being regarded as instrumental to the development of intelligent and moral creatures.' (13)

Tennant's sixth point is that his previous five considerations reinforce one another with cumulative effect. Admittedly each aspect of the universe to which he has drawn attention can, taken separately, be explained without resort to the supernatural. But when we see them together as aspects of a complex universe which is ordered to produce the marvels of animal life, culminating in human intelligence and personality, then in Tennant's view the theistic hypothesis appears as highly plausible and reasonable. The universe might have been a mere formless chaos; but it has form and order, and not only this but an evolving order in which one stage is built upon another to produce in man a consciousness of the universe which also looks beyond it to a transcendent purposive Mind. It is this total fact that demands explanation. And a naturalistic explanation of the details of the creative process merely begs the ultimate question. Tennant insists that 'no *explanation* is contained in the assertion that the world is an organic whole and consequently involves adaptiveness. That is only a restatement of the occult and wondrous fact that cries for explanation. The world's "thusness" is explained, however, if it be attributable to the design and creativeness of a Being whose purpose is, or includes, the realisation of moral values. Further back than a creative Spirit it is neither needful nor possible to go.' (14)

I think that Tennant's argument still stands as the most comprehensive and serious modern restatement of the design argument, and I want presently to discuss it as such, but it will be convenient first to take account of the recent contribution by Richard Taylor, who has presented in a new way the epistemological aspect of the design argument, also stressed by Tennant (see above, p. 19).

(b) Modern restatements: (3) Richard Taylor

As Richard Taylor formulates it, the argument 'rests upon the consideration that our own faculties of sense and cognition are not only remarkable in themselves but are in fact relied upon by us for the discovery of truth': (15)

Suppose then [says Taylor] that you are riding in a railway coach and glancing from the window at one of the stops, you see numerous white stones scattered about on a small hillside near the train in a pattern resembling these letters: THE BRITISH RAILWAYS WELCOMES YOU TO WALES. Now you could scarcely doubt that these stones do not just accidentally happen to exhibit that pattern. You would, in fact, feel quite certain that they were purposefully *arranged* that way to convey an intelligible message. At the same time, however, you could not prove, just from a consideration of their arrangement alone, that they were arranged by a purposeful being. It is possible — at least logically so — that there was no guiding hand at all in back of this pattern, that it is simply the result of the operations of inanimate nature. It is possible that the stones, one by one, rolled down the hill and, over the course of centuries, finally ended up in that interesting arrangement, or that they came in some other accidental way to be so related to each other. For surely the mere fact that something has an interesting or striking shape or pattern, and thus *seems* purposefully arranged, is no proof that it is. . . .

Here, however, is the important point which it is easy to overlook; namely, that *if*, upon seeing from the train window a group of stones arranged as described, you were to conclude that you were entering Wales, and *if* your sole reason for thinking this, whether it was in fact good evidence or not, was that the stones were so arranged, *then* you could not, consistently with that, suppose that the arrangement of the stones was accidental. You would, in fact, be presupposing that they were arranged that way by an intelligent and purposeful being or beings, for the purpose of conveying a certain message having nothing to do with the stones themselves. Another way of expressing

22

the same point is, that it would be *irrational* for you to regard the arrangement of the stones as evidence that you were entering Wales, and at the same time to suppose that they might have come to that arrangement accidentally, that is, as the result of the ordinary interactions of natural or physical forces. (16)

So far Taylor's reasoning is clear. If we believe that marks that can be read as words spelling out an intelligible message have been formed solely by the accidental operation of natural forces, we cannot consistently treat them as the product of a mind which was seeking to convey a message to the reader: we cannot have it both ways. Taylor now applies this principle to the sense organs by which we are aware of the world around us. He points out that 'just as it is possible for a collection of stones to present a novel and interesting arrangement on the side of a hill and [referring to another example which Taylor has used] for marks to appear on a stone in a manner closely resembling some human artefact, and for these things still to be the results of natural, non-purposeful forces, so also it is possible for such things as our own organs of sense to be the accidental and unintended results, over ages of time, of perfectly impersonal, non-purposeful forces.' (17) In fact however we do not treat our sense organs as accidental arrangements of matter, but rather as normally reliable media of information, and just as to take the stones as referring to something is to be taking them as having been intelligently ordered for that purpose, so to take our sense organs as *informing* us about the world is to be taking them to have been deliberately designed to that end:

Just as we supposed that the stones on the hill told us that we were entering Wales — a fact having nothing to do with the stones themselves — so we also suppose that our senses in some manner 'tell us' what is true, at least sometimes. The stones on the hill could, to be sure, have been an accident, in which case we cannot suppose that they really tell us anything at all. So also, our senses and all our faculties could be accidental in their origins, and in that case they do not really tell us anything either. But the fact remains, that we do trust them, without the slightest reflection on the matter. (18)

So Taylor concludes:

> We saw that it would be irrational for anyone to say *both*
> that the marks he found on a stone had a natural, non-
> purposeful origin and *also* that they reveal some truth with
> respect to something other than themselves, something
> that is not merely inferred from them. One cannot
> rationally believe both of these things. So also, it is now
> suggested, it would be irrational for one to say *both* that
> his sensory and cognitive faculties had a natural, non-
> purposeful origin and *also* that they reveal some truth with
> respect to something other than themselves, something
> that is not merely inferred from them. *If* their origin can
> be entirely accounted for in terms of chance variations,
> natural selection, and so on, without supposing that they
> somehow embody and express the purposes of some
> creative being, then the most we can say of them is that
> they exist, that they are complex and wondrous in their
> construction, and are perhaps in other respects interesting
> and remarkable. We cannot say that they are, entirely by
> themselves, reliable guides to any truth whatever, save only
> what can be inferred from their own structure and arrange-
> ment. If, on the other hand, we do assume that they are
> guides to some truths having nothing to do with them-
> selves, then it is difficult to see how we can, consistently
> with that supposition, believe them to have arisen by
> accident, or by the ordinary workings of purposeless
> forces, even over the ages of time. (19)

This is an interesting and thought-provoking but nevertheless, I believe, a fallacious piece of reasoning. Taylor says that
since we treat our sense organs as we treat the words on the
Welsh hillside, namely, as conveying information to us, we
ought to regard our sense organs as we regard 'The British
Railways Welcomes you to Wales', as the work of an intelligent agent. This is the argument. And its weakness is that we
do not treat our sense organs or our sense experience as we
treat a set of words; and therefore consistency does not
require us to think of them, as we think of the words in a
sentence, as having been formed by deliberate intent. We
know that sentences are normally expressions of human

24

intelligence (even though words may occasionally fall into the form of a sentence by pure chance) because we ourselves so use them. But we have no parallel reason to believe that our sense organs are products of an intelligent purpose. On the contrary, the biologists tell us a detailed and convincing story about the way in which the sense organs of the different animal species have been developed through the natural processes of evolution. According to this story the present form, for example, of the human eye as a cognitive organ is a result, not of conscious design on the part of a divine agent, but of the operation over millions of years of the evolutionary mechanism whereby natural selection favours the development of organs that increase the viability of a species.

Taylor is, needless to say, perfectly well aware of the fact of evolution, and of the way in which on the face of it this accounts for the gradual development and improvement of sense organs. He meets this as follows:

> Again, it is sometimes said that the capacity to grasp truths has a decided value to the survival of an organism, and that our cognitive faculties have evolved, quite naturally, through the operation of this principle. This appears far-fetched, however, even if for no other reason than that man's capacity to understand what is true, through reliance upon his senses and cognitive faculties, far exceeds what is needed for survival. One might as well say that the sign on the hill welcoming tourists to Wales originated over the course of ages purely by accident, and has been preserved by the utility it was then found to possess. This is of course possible, but also immensely implausible. (20)

There are two points here. The first is that our human cognitive powers exceed what we should need merely for purposes of survival. Taylor is evidently now speaking, not of our sense organs, but of the higher capacities of the mind for reasoning and speculation, as in the formation of scientific hypotheses and the creation of metaphysical systems. But his design argument was based upon our reliance on our *sense organs* as sources of information; and the counter-argument that these have come about by natural evolution is not met by claiming that our higher intellectual powers have *not* come about in this way. But further, it is by no means implausible to suppose that our higher intellectual powers have in fact developed naturally within the evolutionary process. For there is a continuity on the scale of increasing complexity between the purely pragmatic intelligence which man shares with the apes and other higher vertebrates, and the freer, much more complexly associative and creative intelligence of a scientist or a philosopher. Further, biologists can suggest to us the sorts of factors that must have stimulated the distinctively human development of intelligence — for example, as our ape-like progenitors left the forests for more open country and walked upright their hands became available to use tools; and 'Once our ancestors were using tools, there would have been greater need, and so greater selection, for increased intelligence.' (21) Thus not only the present size and structure of man's brain but also the efforts of thought which it sustains can be seen as growing naturally out of earlier and simpler states, and so as not requiring the hypothesis of a special non-natural creation.

Taylor's second point is the unlikelihood of man's cognitive apparatus having come into its present state 'purely by accident', as the stones on the hillside could (however implausibly) be imagined to have rolled by chance into their present positions. But of course the evolutionary hypothesis does not suggest that the development from a light-sensitive patch on the skin to the complex organisation of the eye happened by chance, but that it happened through a long chain of causes and effects which have taken place in accordance with the observed regularities which we call laws of nature.

In short, just as the most plausible explanation of the arrangement of the stones on the hillside, in the light of the knowledge available to us, is that it is a result of conscious planning, so the most plausible explanation of the structure of our sense organs, in the light of the knowledge available to us, is that they are an outcome of natural evolutionary processes which do not require the postulate of a controlling mind. This difference between the two cases entirely undermines Taylor's new form of design argument. (22)

(c) Theism and probability

We may now return to the central thrust of teleological theistic reasoning as this has been comprehensively formulated by F. R. Tennant. He offers a broadly based probability argument from the character and course of the world, including the emergence within it of the human spirit, to a divine purpose behind the occurrence of such a process. Tennant's position is that theism constitutes our most adequate available explanation of this evolving universe in its totality to the present time. He seeks to show 'that there is a theistic world-view commending itself as more reasonable than other interpretations or than the refusal to interpret, and congruent with the knowledge — i.e. the probability — which is the guide of life and of science'. (23) W. R. Matthews has defined the same enterprise in the following terms: 'given the universe as disclosed in experience, to find the most reasonable account of it. Several hypotheses present themselves for consideration, among them Theism. The question before the mind of the philosopher, therefore, is to decide which of the possible hypotheses squares most adequately with the whole experience of the universe which is open to us. The Theist maintains that his hypothesis is the most rational in this sense.' (24) And again, more cautiously, H. H. Farmer has said of the idea of God that 'it ought, if we bring it *to* the facts of the world, to help us to make sense of them, better sense than, or at least as good sense as, any other available interpretation.' (25) Such advocacy of theism as the most reasonable interpretation of the universe is usually based upon an expansion of the design argument to include among its evidences not only the apparently purposive development of the natural world but also those levels of human experience — aesthetic, moral and religious — which transcend the needs of our animal life. Taking account of the entire range of phenomena, it is claimed, it is more probable that there is a God than that there is not; or (correlatively) it is more reasonable or rational to believe in the reality of God than to disbelieve or to be agnostic. It is this use of probability or likelihood or reasonableness of belief that I want to question, on grounds pointed out by Hume when (pp. 13-14 above) he argued that one cannot make a probability judgement about a unique object such as is the universe in its entirety.

The basic reason for this restriction is that probability is a relational concept, this being equally true whether we think of the probability of events or of the probability of the truth of a proposition.

That a possible event will occur is probable in virtue of its relation to other events. But if the event in question — in this case the occurrence of the universe — is so defined that there can be no other events, then the notion of probability cannot be brought to bear upon it. More specifically, the concept of probability used in the physical and behavioural sciences is based on frequency within a plurality of instances, so that if there is only a single case the concept fails to apply. To claim that the probability of the universe being God-produced is represented by some particular mathematical ratio, $1/n$, would (according to the frequency theory) presuppose it to be known (a) that there is a certain determinate number of universes and (b) that a certain definite proportion of these, namely $1/n$, are God-produced. Not knowing whether our own universe falls within the God-produced or the non-God-produced fraction, we could nevertheless know that the probability of its being God-produced is $1/n$. However, any such use of statistical probability is ruled out by the fact that there is by definition only one universe. For by 'the universe' in this context is meant 'the totality of all that is, apart from any creator of everything other than himself'. It follows from this definition that there is but one universe; and there can accordingly be no ground for a premise to the effect that a certain proportion of universes exhibit a certain characteristic. (26)

Thus Tennant's analogy of the single throw of dice ('Presumably the world is comparable with a single throw of dice. And common sense is not foolish in suspecting the dice to have been loaded.') (27) is merely confusing. For it presupposes a set of prior circumstances, such as that the dice has six faces, in relation to which there is an antecedently calculable probability of a particular number turning up at a single throw.

A similar point arises with regard to propositions. A proposition has probability in virtue of its relation to other

28

evidence-stating propositions. But if a proposition's domain is so wide that nothing remains outside it then, again, the notion of probability cannot apply. But just this seems to be the case with regard to propositions interpreting the universe as a whole. In such a case there is no conceivable background of information on which an estimate of probability could be based. There can be no prior corpus of propositions in relation to which a total interpretation could be judged to be probable or improbable, since all our particular items of information are included within the totality which is being interpreted. There can, in other words, be no evidence in favour of one total interpretation over against another.

What these considerations show is that any notion of probability properly invoked by a comprehensive teleological argument must be other than the usual statistical or logical concept. Tennant is fully aware of this, and indeed argues to the same effect. He considers the view 'that, if the world be the sole instance of its kind, or be analogous to a single throw, there can be no talk of chances or of antecedent probability in connection with our question. Sound as this caution is, [he says] it does not affect the teleologist; for, when he calls coincidence on the vast scale improbable, he has in mind not mathematical probability, or a logical relation, but the alogical probability which is the guide of life and which has been found to be the ultimate basis of all scientific induction.' (28)

Tennant discusses this alogical probability which operates within the theistic judgement (and on which he believes that scientific induction also ultimately rests) and characterises it as 'non-rational, yet reasonable, certitude determined psycho-logically'. (29) His position is I think that when the human mind surveys the universe in which it finds itself, its conviction that this indefinitely complex cosmos could not have come into being in a completely random and unplanned way is a reasonable even though not a logically compelling conviction, reflecting a real implausibility or (alogical) improbability in the chance hypothesis.

But the question still has to be raised whether even this nonmathematical and 'alogical' concept of probability is applicable to the theistic problem. It is of course a fact that as men have looked at the world and have been especially

29

struck by this or that aspect of it they have concluded that there is (or that there is not) a God, or have found in the world confirmation of an already formed conviction as to the existence (or non-existence) of God in terms varying in degree from 'it seems on the whole more likely than not' to 'it is overwhelmingly more probable'. But the question remains whether the notion of probability or likelihood is being used in such judgements to express more than a purely personal and imponderable 'hunch' or feeling.

The situation seems to be this. Of the immense number and variety of apparently relevant considerations some, taken by themselves, point in one direction and some in the other. One group can fairly be said to count as at least prima facie evidence for the existence of God. For not only do believers urge these particular considerations as supporting their own position but disbelievers concurringly treat them as points requiring special explanation. And likewise there are other considerations which taken by themselves constitute at least prima facie antitheistic evidences. These are matters which non-believers emphasise and in which the believer, on the other hand, sees a challenge to his faith which he feels obliged to try to meet.

As examples of prima facie theistic evidence, man's distinctively religious experience and the reports of miracles would never be pointed out by an atheist as tending positively to support his own position; they are items for which he feels the need for an explanation other than the one which the facts themselves, when taken at their face value, suggest. It is agreed for example that there is such a thing as 'religious experience', and this very name embodies a religious interpretation of the experiences in question as being in some way cognitive of the divine. Accordingly it is incumbent upon the disbeliever to respond by offering a naturalistic interpretation of these same experiences. Such reinterpretations have been offered in abundance and have usually followed the path marked out by Thomas Hobbes in his paradigmatic remark that when a man says that God has spoken to him in a dream this 'is no more than to say he dreamed that God spake to him'. (30)

On the other hand, as examples of prima facie antitheistic evidence, human wickedness and the suffering of all sentient creature including man are not facts which would be selected by the theist as favourable premises from which to launch his own argument: they are rather difficulties which he must endeavour to meet from the wider resources of theism, as has been done by a succession of thinkers from Augustine to the present day.

There are yet other factors which are not so manifestly evidential as those already mentioned but which seem nevertheless to fit rather more readily into one conception than the other. For example, moral experience finds readier hospitality within a religious metaphysic, whilst on the other hand the vastness of the physical universe and the insignificant place occupied in it by man can more immediately be assimilated into a naturalistic world-view.

Now none of these factors or of the indefinitely many others that could be added to them points so unequivocally in a particular direction as to admit of only one possible explanation. Although in isolation they each suggest a conclusion, nevertheless each is capable of being fitted into either a religious or a naturalistic context. There is no item offered as theistic or antitheistic evidence which cannot be absorbed by a mind operating with different presuppositions into the contrary view. The question then is whether one *way* of interpreting them can be said to be more probable than the other or (putting the same query in another way) whether acceptance of one interpretation can be said to be more reasonable or rational than acceptance of the other. For the choice is never between explanation and blank lack of explanation, but always between alternative explanations employing radically different categories.

From the fact that there are particular considerations which count as prima facie evidence both for and against theism it follows that if we attend only to selected items we may well receive the impression that the evidence as a whole tends in one direction — *which* direction depending of course upon which items of evidence are central in our thoughts. However, since theism and naturalism can each alike lay claim to prima facie evidences and must each admit the existence of prima facie difficulties, any fruitful comparison must treat the two alternative interpretations as comprehensive wholes, with their distinctive strengths and weaknesses.

In what sense, however, or on what basis can it be claimed to be established that one such total interpretation is more probable than another? Can we, for example, simply count points for and against? Can we say that there are, say, ten items of prima facie evidence in favour of theism and eight against, so that theism wins by two points; or vice versa? Clearly no such mechanical procedure will do, for the conflicting considerations do not form units of equal weight. Can we perhaps however place each item in its position on an evidential scale in which, without being assigned numerical value, they are nevertheless listed in order of importance? To some extent this is feasible as a separate operation on each side of the debate. In many instances we can accord a greater weight to one item of theistic (or of antitheistic) evidence than to another, and can thus at least begin to construct two parallel lists. But we still have no agreed way of weighing an item on one list against its opposite number on the other list nor, therefore, of evaluating one list as a whole in relation to the other. There are no common scales in which to weigh, for example, human wickedness and folly against the fact of man's moral experience, or the phenomenon of Christ against the problem of human and animal suffering. Judgements on such matters are intuitive and personal, and the notion of probability, if it is applied, no longer has any objective meaning.

What is sought to be done here is something which no one has yet succeeded in doing, namely to show by arguments acceptable to all parties that one comprehensive world-view has superior probability to another. The criteria by which to match metaphysical systems against each other which have usually been suggested are those developed in connection with the coherence theory of truth — the internal logical consistency of each system of thought; their explanatory comprehensiveness (so that if one covers data which the other has to leave out of account the former is to that extent superior); and the 'adequacy' with which they illuminate and explain what they profess to explain. The first two of these criteria will not help us at this point, since there are forms both of theism and of naturalism which are internally consistent and which are equally comprehensive in the sense that there are no data that evade their explanatory scope. The issue is, once again, not between explanation and no explanation but between two radically different kinds of explanation. The crucial question is thus whether one way of accounting for the data can be said to be inherently more adequate than the other. This is in effect our original problem as to whether theism or naturalism can meaningfully be said to possess a superior antecedent probability. And it now seems that there is no objective sense in which one consistent and comprehensive word-view can be described as inherently more probable than another. It is of course a truism, if not a tautology, that to the theist theism seems more adequate and that to the naturalist naturalism seems more adequate. But this is because they are judging from importantly different standpoints and with different criteria and presuppositions. And it appears that the issue between them is not one that can be settled by appeal to any agreed procedure or by reference to any objectively ascertainable probabilities.

(d) 'Design' as question rather than answer

I think it is clear, then, that the design argument neither proves the existence of a creative mind behind the physical universe nor in any objective sense shows this to be probable. And yet, as many have pointed out, the response to the complex order of the world expressed in the design argument continues, relatively untroubled by the logical insufficiency of the argument itself. As Kant (who described this proof as 'the oldest, the clearest, and the most accordant with the common reason of mankind') (31) wrote:

> It would therefore not only be uncomforting but utterly vain to attempt to diminish in any way the authority of this argument. Reason, constantly upheld by this ever-increasing evidence, which, though empirical, is yet so powerful, cannot be so depressed through doubts suggested by subtle and abstruse speculation, that it is not at once aroused from the indecision of all melancholy reflection, as from a dream, by one glance at the wonders of nature and the majesty of the universe — ascending from

height to height up to the all-highest, from the conditioned to its conditions, up to the supreme and unconditional Author (of all conditioned being). (32)

The reason, I think, is that the argument focuses our attention upon aspects of the world that evoke a sense of wonder and an awareness of mystery independently of the ratiocinative activity of the mind. Cosmic evolution constitutes a transcendence-suggesting mystery to which religion is a natural response. For all explanation and understanding functions within a given framework of the ultimate facts that there is anything at all; that what exists is a universe instead of a mere chaos; and that it is the particular universe that it is and includes our own questioning minds. Our thoughts normally move within the boundaries set by these ultimate circumstances, exploring the internal structure of our universe and directing our actions in relation to it. But as well as analysing the world we sometimes simply contemplate it and wonder at it, allowing ourselves to be grasped by its mysteriousness. Our thought then moves beyond its customary limits to face an ultimate inexplicable 'given', and to marvel at its unlimitedly intricate and yet coherent character. The ultimate 'given' is an evolving order which has not only produced all the facets of the physical world but also all the qualitative marvels of human experience. And the mystery is that this infinitely complex universe just *is* − it hangs, as it were, unsupported, except by a great question mark. And so the possibility inevitably presents itself that this development of galactic gases to produce the spirit of man is not just a sheer inexplicable given fact, but stems from the only source that we can as minds see as independently self-explanatory, namely purposive mind.

Recent developments in astronomical and cosmological theory have emphasised the mysteriousness of the universe revealed to us by the natural sciences. According, for example, to the 'big bang' theory of the origin of the present state of the universe, the matter composing it was, a large but finite number of years ago, bunched together in a state of maximum density from which it 'exploded' into the still expanding universe in which we find ourselves. If that initial condition was an absolute beginning, we have the mystery of

34

a universe coming into being out of nothing. If on the other hand the present expansion was preceded by a contraction, and so on back in an infinite series of expansions and contractions, then the ultimate character of the universe as a pulsating system does not at all resemble a random state out of which order has randomly emerged. Or if on the other hand the rival 'steady state' theory should be correct, with its corollary of the continuous coming into existence of millions of hydrogen atoms every second to compensate for the attenuation of the universe by expansion, we are again faced with an ultimate system, and a system subject to a mysterious process of repair, rather than with randomness.

Further, the religious hypothesis that the universe is a system designed to produce intelligent personal life now seems more plausible in the light of the widely held view that there is life throughout the universe. It used to be said that it is absurd to see the function of the universe in terms of the emergence of man, who is only a fleeting organic excrescence on the surface of a single planet of a minor star out on the periphery of a medium-sized galaxy. Can we think of the whole universe, whose immensity staggers our imagination, as existing for the sake of this little pin-point of consciousness? But it now seems likely that a very large number, perhaps the majority, of stars have planets, and (on the evidence of our own solar system) that something like one planet in ten is capable of sustaining some form of life. In this case there will be life at varying levels of development on thousands of millions of planets circling stars in uncounted numbers of galaxies. Intelligence will exist, often on much higher levels than our own, all over the universe. It is not, in that case, so implausible to consider the universe as a system designed to produce personal life. For apparently it is a system, rather than a random collocation of matter, and apparently it is producing intelligent personal life at innumerable points throughout its vast extent.

If this complex evolving cosmos does indeed embody a purpose, then its mystery is illumined by that fact; otherwise it presents a problem that has no solution. Thus the ultimately inconclusive reasoning of the 'physico-theological proof' leaves us with a query to which the answer *may* be — God. The question may on the other hand have no answer;

35

3 The Cosmological Argument

(a) The Thomist arguments

In the widest sense of the term, any theistic argument that proceeds from the world to God can be described as cosmological. In this sense all the *a posteriori* arguments are cosmological, including the design argument; and that they do indeed have something important in common is attested by Aquinas, who saw his five Ways, the last of which is teleological, as variations on a single basic theme. However, for expository purposes the term 'cosmological' has commonly been restricted either more narrowly to the argument from the contingency of the world (Aquinas's third Way), or — more usefully and less narrowly — to the family of arguments which proceed by means of the principle of sufficient reason from the non-self-explanatory character of the universe to a being whose existence is self-explanatory.

The central thought of the cosmological argument in this latter sense has been well expressed by Leibniz:

Let us suppose the book of the elements of geometry to have been eternal, one copy always having been written down from an earlier one; it is evident that, even though a reason can be given for the present book out of a past one, nevertheless out of any number of books taken in order going backwards we shall never come upon a full reason; though we might well always wonder why there should have been such books from all time — why there were books at all, and why they were written in this manner. What is true of the books is true also of the different states of the world; for what follows is in some way copied from what precedes (even though there are certain laws of change). And so, however far you go back to earlier states, you will never find in those states a full reason why there should be any world rather than none, and why it should be such as it is. (1)

37

We have a classic statement of three forms of cosmological argument in the first three of Aquinas's five Ways; and if we now look at these, and try with the aid of contemporary neo-Thomist philosophers to restate them in their strongest form, it will become clear that they all hinge upon the 'principle of sufficient reason', which we shall then have to examine more closely.

The first Way, derived directly from Aristotle (2), is from the fact of motion or, more generally, from the fact of change, to a prime mover. (Accordingly it is sometimes called the kinetological argument.) Aquinas's exposition is as follows:

Some things in the world are certainly in process of change: this we plainly see. Now anything in process of change is being changed by something else. This is so because it is characteristic of things in process of change that they do not yet have the perfection towards which they move, though able to have it; whereas it is characteristic of something causing change to have that perfection already. For to cause change is to bring into being what was previously only able to be, and this can only be done by something that already is: thus fire, which is actually hot, causes wood, which is able to be hot, to become actually hot, and in this way causes change in the wood. Now the same thing cannot at the same time be both actually x and potentially x, though it can be actually x and potentially y: the actually hot cannot at the same time be potentially hot, though it can be potentially cold. Consequently, a thing in process of change cannot itself cause that same change; it cannot change itself. Of necessity therefore anything in process of change is being changed by something else. Moreover, this something else, if in process of change, is itself being changed by yet another thing; and this last by another. Now we must stop somewhere, otherwise there will be no first cause of the change, and, as a result, no subsequent causes. For it is only when acted upon by the first cause that the intermediate causes will produce the change: if the hand does not move the stick, the stick will not move anything else. Hence one is bound to arrive at some first cause of change

38

not itself being changed by anything, and this is what everybody understands by God. (3)

Motus, 'motion' or 'change', includes not only movement from one place to another (local motion) but also change of size, as when a tree grows bigger or a candle smaller, and change of state (alteration), as when a green leaf becomes brown or a piece of iron becomes red-hot. (4) The latter is for Aquinas the more fundamental mode of change, and is understood in Aristotelian terms as the actualising of a potentiality. Iron is potentially hot, and for a piece of iron to become hot is for that potentiality to be realised. But potentialities are not self-actualising. Iron does not become hot by itself: its capacity to become hot is only realised when fire or some other source of heat is applied to it. Actual heat, in the fire, can actualise the iron's potentiality for heat; but if the world did not already contain actual heat, potentiality for heat could never become actualised. In other words, to change is to be changed: change presupposes an operating cause. But that prior causative activity likewise presupposes a cause; and that, one prior to it; and so on. The regress must either be infinite or must terminate in an 'unmoved mover', an original source of change, whose activity does not pre-suppose a yet prior mover but who (or which) possesses intrinsically the power to produce change. Aquinas rules out the idea of an infinite regress and is thus able to conclude that there must be 'some first cause of change not itself being changed by anything, and this is what everybody understands by God'.

The main steps of the argument are thus:

1. Whatever changes from being potentially x (for example, potentially hot, or potentially at a certain place, or potentially twice its present size) to being actually x is changed by something else.

2. That 'something else' must be actually x.

3. There cannot be an infinite regress of such 'something else's', and therefore there must be an ultimate source of change which does not, in order to operate, require to be moved by something else.

Each of these steps is highly debatable. The last has frequently been questioned, and the questioning of it has led

39

(as we shall see presently) to a neo-Thomist tendency to assimilate the first Way to the third, in which the appeal to the principle of sufficient reason is most explicit. The first two steps have less often been attacked. However in his recent book on 'The Five Ways' Anthony Kenny effectively challenges them both. (5)

In the case of the first, Kenny points out that there is a gap in the reasoning. Aquinas was anxious to exclude the possibility that things are self-moving, and he produced a series of Aristotelian arguments to show that if they are moved they must be moved by something external to them ('Summa contra Gentiles', I 13). But he did not consider the possibility that some things are in movement without being or having been moved, whether by something else or by themselves. Kenny points out that *movetur* covers both of the meanings which are distinguished in English by 'is moving' and 'is being moved'. And he suggests that this ambiguity of the Latin may possibly account for Aquinas's failure to state, and to argue for, the additional premise required by his argument that 'whatever is moving is being moved'. (6) For unless this is established it remains possible that some things are just naturally — and conceivably eternally — in motion (in accordance with Newton's first law) without being *caused* to move at all. Thus the possibility that the physical universe has had no initial state and consists eternally of matter in motion has to be excluded before the first Way can lead anywhere.

As regards the second step — that only something that is actually *x* can cause something else to move from being potentially to being actually *x* — Kenny points out that this holds in some cases but not in others. It is true enough, for example, that a wet towel will not dry you. And until the discovery of electricity it was reasonably believed that only something hot can make another thing hot; but now we are familiar with temperatureless currents of electricity making wires hot. Again, 'a kingmaker need not himself be king, and it is not dead men who commit murders.' (7) Further, it does not require something at the south pole to move things to the south pole. (Otherwise how did the first explorer ever get there?) And 'Applied to change in size, the principle seems even more inapplicable. A man who fattens oxen need not

40

himself be fat.' (8) In short, Aquinas's second premise is not generally enough true to sustain his argument.

When we turn to the third step — the exclusion of an infinite regress — we have to consider whether this is a regress of causes stretching backwards in time or a regress of simultaneous causal conditions. Aquinas's own example of the stick moving, say, a stone and being itself moved by the hand, which is in turn moved by . . . suggests the latter type of regress. So do his Aristotelian arguments against an infinite regress in 'Summa contra Gentiles', I 13. In any case a first Way argument based on the idea of a temporal regress to God would lack cogency for the modern mind, which sees no *a priori* impossibility in the idea of a temporally as well as spatially unbounded universe. And indeed it was one of Aquinas's more controversial contributions to theological discussion in his own day to maintain that the non-eternity of the world cannot be established by demonstrative argument but is known by faith on the basis of revelation. (9) It will therefore be proper to interpret the argument here in non-temporal terms, as is done by a number of modern neo-Thomists. According to this interpretation the infinite regress that is excluded is a regress of simultaneous causal conditions. (10) For an infinite chain of necessary causal conditions would still not *explain* the original phenomenon. In an analogy which some contemporary Thomist writers have used, you do not explain the movement of a railway truck along the track by saying that it is being pulled by another truck in front of it, which is in turn being pulled by one in front of it, and so one, unless you add that the whole line of trucks is being pulled by something which moves without itself having to be moved by anything else — the self-moving mover being in this case the engine. Or again, we can explain the movement of one of the wheels in a watch by showing how it gears in with another wheel by which it is being moved. But however numerous may be the wheels, each moved by another, no multiplicity of them will explain how this arrangement of wheels comes to be in motion. To account for this we have to refer to something else, namely the spring, which imparts movement to the whole system.

Thus the infinite regress which Aquinas excludes when he says that 'we must stop somewhere' is not a chain of effects and causes stretching backwards in time but a regress of causally explanatory circumstances. The railway trucks and the cogs in a watch all move at the same time in moving one another; and to extend their number, even to infinity, would still leave their motion ultimately unexplained. To account for this we have to postulate an independent source of motion which originates the series of movements, regardless of whether the series is finite or infinite. And likewise in the case of the universe as a complex interrelated process. We do not explain the fact of change merely by tracing out its moving patterns either in the present or into the past. If the fact of universal process is to be ultimately intelligible it must be seen to depend upon a spontaneous source of motion outside the system itself.

Aquinas's second Way, the first cause (or aetiological) argument, is as follows:

> The second way is based on the nature of causation. In the observable world causes are found to be ordered in series; we never observe, nor ever could, something causing itself, for this would mean it preceded itself, and this is not possible. Such a series of causes must however stop somewhere; for in it an earlier member causes an intermediate and the intermediate a last (whether the intermediate be one or many). Now if you eliminate a cause you also eliminate its effects, so that you cannot have a last cause, nor an intermediate one, unless you have a first. Given therefore no stop in the series of causes, and hence no effect, and this would be an open mistake. One is therefore forced to suppose some first cause, to which everyone gives the name 'God'. (11)

At first sight it is rather harder, as a matter of exegesis, to interpret this in the modern neo-Thomist manner, because Aquinas uses the word 'cause' in a sense which suggests that a cause precedes its effect in time: an event could not cause itself, he says, 'for this would mean it preceded itself'. And so he argues that a present effect must have had a prior cause, which must in turn have had a prior cause, and so backwards either in an infinite regress or to the point at which the temporal series was launched by an uncaused cause. However

42

if we understand the argument in this way it has very little plausibility. For it is not evident that the causal sequence, or rather complex of interlocking sequences, may not extend indefinitely into the past without ever reaching an initial state.

However *prius* does not necessarily mean temporally prior; it may mean logically prior. (12) And so as in the case of the first Way, the argument can be restated in non-temporal terms. It is then a variation on the theme of the first Way. 'We are not', says Eric Mascall, 'arguing about a chain of causes stretching back into the past, but about a chain of causes existing in the present and each depending on the one beyond.' (13) And F. C. Copleston offers in illustration the fact that a person's present activity is causally dependent upon (or has as a necessary condition) the existence of the air which he is breathing; and this in turn is causally dependent upon other wider physical conditions, and these upon others. We thus have 'a hierarchy of causes, in which a subordinate member is here and now dependent on the causal activity of a higher member'. (14)

This series of necessary conditions must either be infinite or depend upon a first cause which is not itself dependent upon a yet prior cause. In this interpretation the motive power of the argument is the need to *explain* the universe. As Copleston says of the series of movers or causes in the first two Ways, 'unless there is a "first" member, a mover which is not itself moved or a cause which does not itself depend on the causal activity of a higher cause, it is not possible to explain the "motion" or the causal activity of the lowest member.' (15) The essence of the argument is thus that if reality is not to be ultimately inexplicable it must include a being whose existence is self-explanatory, in relation to which the existence of everything else can be understood.

The third Way rests upon the same basic principle of explanatoriness or sufficient reason. Aquinas's text is as follows:

Some of the things we come across can be but need not be, for we find them springing up and dying away, thus sometimes in being and sometimes not. Now everything cannot be like this, for a thing that need not be, once was not; and

43

if everything need not be, once upon a time there was nothing. But if that were true there would be nothing even now, because something that does not exist can only be brought into being by something already existing. So that if nothing was in being nothing could be brought into being, and nothing would be in being now, which contradicts observation. Not everything therefore is the sort of thing that need not be; there has got to be something that must be. Now a thing that must be, may or may not owe this necessity to something else. But just as we must stop somewhere in a series of causes, so also in the series of things which must be and owe this to other things. One is forced therefore to suppose something which must be, and owes this to no other thing than itself; indeed it itself is the cause that other things must be. (16)

Once again, the argument can be strengthened by removing the reference to time. The idea that if each existing thing has a beginning then there must have been a time in the past when nothing existed is clearly fallacious. (17) For the world might consist of a beginningless stream of events (or 'things'), each individually having a beginning and an end but overlapping in such a way that there is no time when none of them exists. However if, with the modern neo-Thomists, we see the third Way as being concerned with the *intelligibility* of the world, then the reference to a 'time when nothing existed' can be dispensed with. The argument begins by pointing to the fact of contingency — that is, the fact that there are (at least) some things which 'can be but need not be'. The existence of such a thing does not constitute a self-explanatory fact. In order to find it intelligible under the principle of sufficient reason we have to look beyond it to other circumstances by reference to which its existence is explained. For example, the existence of the tennis ball on the road is explained by the facts that there is a tennis court on the other side of the fence and that the ball has been hit too hard and has landed on the road. But then the existence of the court and of the game being played on it are likewise contingent facts, explicable only by reference beyond themselves. To explain the existence of the tennis court we have to refer to the people who made it, whose existence was in turn dependent on that of their parents, and so on back down the generations and down the evolutionary stream; and to explain the existence of the site and the materials we have to refer to the structure of the earth, and then to its formation, and then to the formation of the solar system. These explanatory regresses, taken far enough, meet in the complex fact of the spatio-temporal universe as a whole. But this also is not a self-explanatory phenomenon. It is not self-evident that matter, with the properties that it has, must exist or that it must be ordered as it is. The existence of the physical universe with its particular structure, although so enormously vaster and more complex a fact, is as much in need of explanation as was the existence of the tennis ball on the road. And if we suppose, as we well may, that the universe is both spatially and temporally unlimited and has had no beginning, its existence with the concrete character that it has is still not *explained*. It is merely pointed to as a uniquely comprehensive fact. There is no evident *reason* why the universe should not consist of empty space; or of half, or twice, as much matter as it does; or why such laws as the conservation of energy or such basic characteristics as the speed of light should obtain. The existence of the universe — that is, the existence of space-time structured as it is, and of matter with the properties that it has — is a sheer given 'brute' fact. And to apply to it the principle of sufficient reason is to see it as a contingent fact, pointing beyond itself for the ground of its intelligibility.

If then — the cosmological argument claims — the existence of the universe is an ultimately intelligible fact, it must be so by reference to a reality whose existence and character is self-explanatory and whose relation to the space-time universe provides a sufficient reason for the latter's existence. And this, as Aquinas says at the end of several of his 'Ways', is what we mean by God.

In the third Way passage itself there is another turn to the argument before this conclusion is reached. Having shown that there must be a necessary being, Aquinas adds, 'Now a thing that must be, may or may not owe this necessity to something else. But just as we must stop somewhere in a series of causes, so also in the series of things which must be and owe this to other things.' Thus he thinks it possible for

45

there to be a number of necessary beings. What does he have in mind? The answer is that angels, human souls and the heavenly bodies were for Aquinas necessary beings in virtue of the fact that they were by nature immortal. But whilst Aquinas calls these things necessary, nevertheless they clearly do not possess the unqualified necessity of the divine nature. Although Aquinas does not put the distinction in this way, one respect in which they differ from God is that whereas he exists eternally, they only exist sempiternally — i.e. they have a beginning but (apart from divine annihilation) no end. However the introduction of these sempiternals does not affect the outcome of the third Way argument; for they depend for their existence upon a creator, and if this creator is himself sempiternal he too must depend upon a creator ... and the regress ends in a being who is necessary in the absolute sense of existing without beginning or end. It is this that 'all men call God'.

(b) The self-explanatory and the non-self-explanatory

Understood in this way the argument hinges upon the claim that the space-time continuum, as a contingent, non-self-explanatory phenomenon only becomes intelligible when seen in relation to an eternal self-existent being who has established it. Let us call this claim, which is the nerve of this family of arguments, the cosmological principle. More briefly it is the premise that the existence of God would be self-explanatory, whereas the existence of the physical universe is not. But this principle can be and has been challenged. Would not an eternal self-existent deity constitute as sheerly and starkly 'given' a fact as an eternal realm of matter or energy? Antony Flew insists that 'Facts about God, however important, do not thereby cease to be, simply, facts. ... No reason whatever has yet been given for considering that God would be an inherently more intelligible ultimate than — say — the most fundamental laws of energy and stuff.' (18) I think that Flew is right in complaining that cosmological arguers have often been content to treat as intuitively evident the principle that the existence of an eternal creative Mind would be self-explanatory in a way in which the existence of the physical universe, exhibiting the fundamental laws which

46

it does exhibit, would not. He is right to want to have the grounds of this principle produced. And indeed the exploration of these grounds is perhaps the most interesting part of an examination of the cosmological argument today, when its inner principle has been explicitly questioned. I think it will appear, on the one hand, that the cosmological principle is not capable of demonstrative proof but, on the other hand, that it has a certain inevitability as an expression of the fact that to us as conscious beings the fact of conscious mental existence is not a candidate for explanation as is the fact of the physical universe. It is only with an effort that we can temporally suspend this very natural prejudice built into our nature. It has a status comparable with that of the 'natural beliefs' — such as our acceptance of the independent existence of the perceived world — to which Hume drew attention. And accordingly a defence of the cosmological principle will consist in displaying its deep roots in this ground of natural or commonsense judgement.

But first it will be well to formulate more precisely the issue to which this principle is relevant. It is not a response to the very peculiar problem (perhaps a product of language when it is idling), Why is there something rather than nothing? For that there is something is a circumstance than which there could be none more ultimate by which to explain it. We can only accept as a given starting-point for thought the fact that 'something is'. But whilst to seek an explanation of the fact that anything at all exists would be to seek for what cannot be, to seek an explanation of the fact that what exists is as it is rather than otherwise is a logically permissible project. Indeed the assumption that there is always a reason (whether or not we can know it) why the universe or any bit of it is at a given time thus rather than otherwise has been dignified with the name of the Principle of Sufficient Reason. (19) This principle cannot be demonstrated; but it is presupposed by so many of the processes of thought which we call rational as itself to count as a fundamental principle of rationality. To reject it seriously and in practice would probably lead to one being certified as insane, and certainly to one's opting out of all forms of rational inquiry. To operate the principle of sufficient reason, then, is to look for explanations; and we must now notice how this

47

process of explaining proceeds. To explain a puzzling phenomenon is to set it in a wider context, or in connection with some further circumstance, in relation to which it is no longer puzzling. But one may of course then be puzzled by this explanation-providing situation, and consider how it in turn is explained. However in such a process something must in the end be left unexplained, namely that ultimate state of affairs which is not related to anything yet more ultimate, by which it might itself be rendered intelligible. If there is something (such as the universe) so comprehensive that it can have no wider context, or something (such as a creator of everything that exists other than himself) of such a nature that there is nothing that could stand in an explanatory relation to it, then this thing will *de facto* terminate the explanatory process.

Now as *de facto* ultimates, God and the physical universe enjoy an equal status; and observing this fact, many critics of the cosmological argument have concluded that it lacks all force. But we are only now approaching a view of the special feature of our situation to which the cosmological argument points. For it alleges that the idea of God provides a *de jure* as well as a *de facto* terminus to the explanatory process. That is to say the idea of God is the idea of a self-explanatory reality, or better, of an entity which is ultimate within a kind (namely consciousness) which we, being ourselves of this kind, accept as not requiring explanation in terms of anything of a different kind.

Thus the two contentions involved in the cosmological principle are (a) that the existence of the physical universe itself, with its fundamental laws of energy, is not something which anyone can on reflection regard as self-explanatory, and (b) that the idea of God can very naturally and reasonably be regarded as exhibiting self-explanatoriness. Both of these contentions must now be given supporting commentary.

As regards the first, we can conceive that the universe might have been very different. The fundamental laws of matter might have been otherwise. The law of gravitation, for instance, which has contributed to making possible the evolution of matter to produce solar systems and life, might not have obtained. Indeed there might have been no universe

48

at all in the sense of an orderly arrangement of matter. And because we can conceive of matter-energy displaying a fundamentally different character, we are left with the question — whether or not we can answer it — as to *why* matter is in fact disposed as it is rather than otherwise.

Now in the application of the principle of sufficient reason it is quite acceptable, and indeed by no means unusual, to cross the category boundary between the mental and the physical. We frequently accept as valid a reference to minds and their purposes and activities in explanation of the dispositions of matter. For example, when we see a moving object — say a car travelling along a road, — if we find that we are able to explain its movement by reference to human intelligence and volition we do not look any further. We take it that we have arrived at a real explanation of the fact that the car is moving along the road. (Not of *how* it is moving — by what system of combustion in cylinders connected with rods and wheels — but of *why* all this is going on, rather than not going on, in that place at that time.) In this case we treat mind as a reality of a higher order in the explanatory hierarchy than matter. And indeed, as minds, we inevitably generalise this principle. It is true that we know of plenty of instances in which the prior behaviour of matter determines the dispositions of mind — as when a rock hits someone on the head and renders him confused or unconscious. But this does not vitiate the general priority of mind over matter, from the point of view of mind, in the explanatory hierarchy. In the case of our car driver we may of course pursue the explanation indefinitely further within the realm of consciousness and intention. We can ask why he was driving along that road at that time; and if it was in order to keep a business appointment we can ask why he wanted to do this; and so on. But we shall not thereby repeat the kind of move that we made when we turned from matter to mind for the explanation of the car's being where it was and moving as it did. We shall not be appealing to a reality of a yet higher order than mind in the explanatory hierarchy. Indeed we cannot conceive of any further order of reality in terms of which mind might itself be explained. We can readily conceive of superior minds to ourselves; but not of kinds of reality superior to mind. Thus there is for us an explanatory

49

ultimacy about mind which we do not find in the existence or the laws of matter. As minds we do not ask why there should be any such thing as mind, although we do ask why there should be any such thing as matter obeying the particular laws which we find matter to obey.

This explanatory ultimacy of mind for minds, or inevitable prejudice of mind in its own favour as an intrinsically intelligible kind of entity, may be said to place the cosmological principle among the 'natural beliefs' to which humanity tends spontaneously to assent. As conscious minds we can accept the existence of purposive intelligence as an ultimate fact, neither requiring nor permitting explanation in terms of anything more ultimate than itself. We can accordingly conceive that the structuring of matter as it is and the consequent course that its evolution has taken are explicable by reference to a creative divine Mind; and no further question then arises as to why that divine Mind should exist. As minds, we can rest in the thought of an eternal and infinite self-existent Mind behind the contingent phenomena of a physical universe within which our own finite minds have emerged.

This then is the kind of support — not demonstration — of which the cosmological principle is capable. Although no one is logically obliged to accept it, yet the principle is so entirely natural an expression of man's own self-awareness that to adopt it cannot be regarded as in any way irrational. There is thus, for many people at least, force in the dilemma proposed by the cosmological argument: either the existence of the universe, ordered as it is, is explicable by reference to God, or it is not explicable at all but remains a sheer brute fact fruitlessly provoking the question, Why should it be? Hence it is both a logically permissible and a very natural view that *if* the existence of the universe, as an ordered cosmos, is ultimately explicable or intelligible it must be so in virtue of its dependence upon an eternal self-existent reality which is of the same order as conscious mind.

It seems to me — differing here from Flew — that an atheist could perfectly well accept this cosmological principle. That is to say, he could agree that *if* there is an eternal, self-existent creative Mind responsible for the existence of the physical universe, with the concrete

50

character that it has, then the question, Why does the universe exist? would have an answer, and an answer in terms of something which we can accept as having being in its own right and not requiring a *raison d'être* referring beyond itself. But having agreed that the universe is either unexplained or is to be explained theistically, he would add that there is no reason here to adopt the latter alternative. There is no adequate reason to do other than accept the universe as simply an ultimate inexplicable datum. For whilst the cosmological argument presents us with the options: universe as brute fact or as divine creation, it does not provide any ground for preferring one to the other.

And of the two the more economical option is the atheistic one. Thus in a celebrated debate between Bertrand Russell and F. C. Copleston, in which a cosmological argument and an atheistic response to it are clearly displayed, Copleston urges that if there is no God the universe is (as the atheist existentialist, Sartre, said) 'gratuitous'; and Russell, rejecting the term 'gratuitous', replies 'I should say that the universe is just there, and that's all.' (20) And with this acceptance by Russell of the world itself as an ultimate datum their dialogue reaches an impasse. In another discussion of the argument from contingency, Copleston acknowledges in effect that Russell's position is unassailable. He says:

> One can hardly admit that the existence of a finite being at all constitutes a serious problem and at the same time maintain that the solution can be found anywhere else than in affirming the existence of the transfinite. If one does not wish to embark on the path which leads to the affirmation of transcendent being, however the latter may be described (if it is described at all), one has to deny the reality of the problem, assert that things 'just are' and that the existential problem in question is a pseudo-problem. And if one refuses even to sit down at the chess-board and make a move, one cannot, of course, be check-mated. (21)

And this, it seems to me, is where the cosmological argument leaves us. It points very clearly to the possibility of God as the ground of the ultimate intelligibility of the universe in which we find ourselves, and of ourselves as part of it. But in

4 Moral Arguments

(a) God as a postulate of practical reason

The modern attempt to show that God is known through or is implied by man's moral experience begins with Immanuel Kant, who in his 'Critique of Practical Reason' argued that the existence of God is a postulate of the practical or moral reason. In his 'Critique of Pure Reason' Kant had attacked the prevailing rationalist view, as represented by such thinkers as Leibniz and Wolff, that the reality of God both requires and is capable of logical demonstration. Kant examined the traditional theistic arguments and maintained that the cosmological and teleological presuppose the ontological proof and cannot stand if it falls; and he subjected the ontological proof to powerful and penetrating criticisms which have ever since been widely regarded as fatal to it (see pp. 81-2). Thus for Kant the existence of God is not something that in the strict sense of the term we can *know*. This does not however mean that we are not entitled to believe it. For as well as being a theorising intellect man is a moral agent, in touch with reality as it impinges upon him as an ethical being. When the practical reason finds it necessary to believe something Kant does not speak of knowledge but of faith *(Glaube)*; and one outcome of the critical inquiry by which he defined the limits of theoretical reason was to 'deny knowledge, in order to make room for faith.' (1) This *Glaube* takes the form of the postulation by practical reason of certain metaphysical facts which are presupposed in its own operation: namely human freedom, human immortality and the existence of God.

How does Kant arrive at this conclusion in the case of the existence of God?

It is a fundamental principle of his ethical thinking that 'It is impossible to conceive anything at all in the world, or even out of it, which can be taken as good without qualification, except a good will'. (2) But whilst the good will, or virtue, is

53

the only thing that is intrinsically good, in that it is good in all possible circumstances, and is thus the highest good in one sense of that term *(summum* in the sense of *supremum)*, it is nevertheless not the highest good in the sense of the perfect or most complete good *(summum* in the sense of *consummatum*). This latter, identified by Christianity with the Kingdom of God, (3) would be the best possible state of affairs, and must as such consist in more than moral goodness. For if all men were virtuous but were also in pain and misery, their virtue would still be intrinsically valuable but nevertheless the total situation would not be the best possible. The *summum bonum,* in its most comprehensive sense, would still remain unrealised. That requires not only moral goodness but also the crowning of it with happiness. 'For to be in need of happiness and also worthy of it and yet not to partake of it could not be in accordance with the complete volition of an omnipotent rational being. . . .' (4) In other words, reason approves as the only rationally satisfying state of affairs one in which moral goodness exists and is appropriately correlated with happiness.

Kant does not argue directly from these premises to the existence of God, but claims that divine existence is a postulate, or presupposition, of the claim of morality upon us. His reasoning can be set out as follows.

First, the ultimate object of a good will — that which a good will seeks to bring about as far as it is able — is the *summum bonum,* or perfect state of affairs: 'the highest good is the necessary highest end of a morally determined will and a true object thereof'. (5) In short, it is 'our duty to promote the highest good'. (6)

Second, since 'ought' implies 'can', it follows from the fact that it is the good will's duty to try to bring about the highest good that it is possible for that highest good to come about. Thus it is 'a necessity connected with duty as a requisite to presuppose the possibility of this highest good'. (7)

Third, although the realisation of the highest good must thus be possible, it is not within *our* power as finite beings to bring it about. We are free to achieve virtue in ourselves, but not to ensure that happiness is added to virtue, thus realising the perfect state of affairs.

54

Fourth, there must consequently be a rational and moral being who as creator and ruler of the world has the power to bring moral desert and happiness into harmony with one another. Therefore 'the existence is postulated of a cause of the whole of nature, itself distinct from nature, which contains the ground of the exact coincidence of happiness with morality'. (8)

Further, since the apportioning of happiness to virtue does not take place in this life it must be attained in eternity, (9) and so the postulate of immortality (for which Kant has already argued on the ground that the obligation to attain perfect goodness can only be met by an infinite progress towards perfection, which in turn requires infinite time for its occurrence) is closely connected with the postulate of divine existence.

The exact status of these postulates (together with the third postulate of human freedom) in Kant's thought is not easy to determine. They do not constitute knowledge, i.e. they are not established conclusions of theoretical reason; although on the other hand the theoretical intellect has no reason to resist or reject them. (10) What, I think, Kant means is that to take our ethical nature fully seriously, accepting moral obligations as having objective and binding validity, is to presuppose that the universe in which we exist has a particular character, the basic features of which are indicated by the metaphysical postulates of God, freedom and immortality.

However Kant's reasoning, as regards the postulate of divine existence, is open to criticism. It is a turning-point of his argument that the *summum bonum* (consisting of virtue rewarded with happiness) is possible, and that in order for it to be possible God must exist as a moral and omnipotent Being. But what does 'possible' mean in this context? It may merely mean 'logically possible'. But in order for the *summum bonum* to be possible in this sense it is not necessary either that the ideal state of affairs should ever actually come about or therefore that a Being should exist with the power to bring it about. All that is required is that the concept of the *summum bonum* be not self-contradictory. Thus the mere logical possibility of the *summum bonum* cannot require us to postulate divine existence. Accordingly Kant's argument demands that when we affirm the *summum bonum* to be possible we are affirming it to be factually (and not merely logically) possible.

Now one ground on which, according to Kant, a state of affairs can be known to be factually possible is that someone is under a moral obligation to bring it about. For 'ought' implies 'can'; so that if I ought to create a certain state of affairs it follows that I can create it, and therefore that it can exist. The question, then, is, Who is under a moral obligation to realise the *summum bonum*? Clearly we cannot at this point suggest God as the answer; for it is God whose existence we are seeking grounds for affirming. It must then be man. But it is an essential part of Kant's argument that man himself does *not* have the power to bring about the *summum bonum* — for which reason we have to postulate God. Man's obligation is to do all that he can towards the realisation of the *summum bonum*. But the *summum bonum* contains two distinct elements — the existence of good wills, and the proportioning of happiness to desert — such that either could be realised without the other. It could be the case that there is moral goodness, but no correlation between the good will and good fortune: and conversely it could be the case that good fortune is distributed according to moral desert but that no good wills exist. And our obligation to do all we can to realise the *summum bonum* is an obligation to become good wills; from which it follows that it is possible for us to do so. We are not however under obligation to bring about the second part of the *summum bonum,* for this is not within our power; and therefore there is no implication, from any obligation lying upon us, concerning the factual possibility of this second part or, accordingly, of the *summum bonum* as a whole. Nor therefore is there any proper ground in our moral duty for postulating the existence of God as the agent necessary to bring about the *summum bonum*.

(b) The post-Kantian type of moral argument

In Idealist philosophy and theology since Kant the moral

56

argument for the existence of God has been deployed in various ways by a large number of thinkers. We may take as representative the version offered by Hastings Rashdall in his 'The Theory of Good and Evil' (1907). Rashdall freely recognised that a man might be moved by a moral ideal, and might live by its behests, whilst forming no beliefs, or only negative beliefs, concerning the ultimate source and status of that ideal. But, Rashdall says, 'the question arises whether, when the attempt to harmonize and so to justify our beliefs is honestly made, the man who wishes to defend and rationalize his practical recognition of moral obligation may not be forced into the alternative of giving up his ethical creed or of giving up certain views of the Universe which reflection has shown to be inconsistent with that creed.' (11)

The starting-point of Rashdall's argument is thus the 'absoluteness' or 'objectivity' of moral obligation. This, he assumes, is something which the agnostic will agree in affirming. 'The truth', he says, 'that the moral ideal is what it is whether we like it or not is the most essential element in what the popular consciousness understands by "moral obligation". Moral obligation means moral objectivity. That *at least* seems to be implied in any legitimate use of the term: at least it implies the existence of an absolute, objective moral ideal.' (12) The problem, then, is how to conceive the nature of the universe consistently with the reality of objective moral values and laws. At this point Rashdall launches his main argument:

> We say that the Moral Law has a real existence, that there is such a thing as an absolute Morality, that there is something absolutely true or false in ethical judgements, whether we or any number of human beings at any given time actually think so or not. . . . We must therefore face the question *where* such an ideal exists, and what manner of existence we are to attribute to it. Certainly it is to be found, wholly and completely, in no individual human consciousness. . . . Only if we believe in the existence of a Mind for which the true moral ideal is already in some sense real, a Mind which is the source of whatever is true in our own moral judgements, can we rationally think of the moral ideal as no less real than the world itself. Only so

57

can we believe in an absolute standard of right and wrong, which is as independent of this or that man's actual ideas and actual desires as the facts of material nature. The belief in God ... is the logical presupposition of an 'objective' or absolute Morality. A moral ideal can exist nowhere and nohow but in a mind; an absolute moral ideal can exist only in a Mind from which all Reality is derived. (13) Our moral ideal can only claim objective validity in so far as it can rationally be regarded as the revelation of a moral ideal eternally existing in the mind of God. (14)

Clearly the argument hinges upon the 'objectivity' of moral values and laws, that is to say, upon their independence of the human minds which become conscious of them. If moral values do indeed have such a status then Rashdall's argument is well on the way to its conclusion, which in effect gives the name 'God' to the independent source and ground of ethics. But the 'objectivity' of morality is not the uncontroversial premise that Rashdall seems to have assumed. On the contrary, the agnostic (or humanist, to use the term more generally preferred today) denies it and offers instead a purely naturalistic account of the origin and nature of moral values. We shall look at a particular naturalistic ethical theory — that of Bertrand Russell — presently. But nearly all such theories follow a common basic pattern. Man, it is pointed out, is a gregarious animal; and human beings cannot live together successfully in societies without obeying rules of behaviour which harmonise their interests. Such rules, gradually developed through the experience of group existence, are internalised by social conditioning in the form of moral ideals and obligations. They owe their felt 'absoluteness' and 'objectivity' to the tremendous power and authority of the clan over the individual members whose moral outlook and habits it has moulded from birth. This accounts for the feeling that conscience represents a divine 'voice' whose commands and prohibitions we must obey — a feeling which various nineteenth-century thinkers, in particular, developed into a form of moral argument for the existence of God. Cardinal J. H. Newman, for example, wrote: 'If, as is the case, we feel responsibility, are ashamed, are frightened, at transgressing the voice of conscience, this implies that there is One to whom we are responsible, before whom we are ashamed, whose claim upon us we fear.' (15) But from the naturalistic point of view Newman was misreading the internalised requirements of our social nature, generated entirely by the circumstances of the life of the human animal, as the commands of a supernatural Being.

(c) A reformulated moral argument

We have not thus far found any proof moving from man's moral experience to the existence of a supreme being. Nor, I believe, is it possible to find one. But nevertheless the fact of moral obligation, even on a naturalistic meta-ethical analysis, can, I think, present a fatal challenge to a humanist philosophy; and I should like now to formulate this challenge. I shall suggest that a humanist who performs an act of extreme self-sacrifice for the good of humanity is thereby presupposing the falsity of his professed beliefs. From the point of view of his creed — I shall argue — his action is irrational; whilst in relation to his action his creed is inadequate.

Let us consider the case — the admittedly extreme case — of the humanist who knowingly sacrifices his life for the sake of humanity as a whole. We are thus thinking of self-sacrifice on moral principle rather than of the rather different case of the impulsive self-giving of one who loses his life whilst, for example, trying to save a child from drowning; or the different case again of the soldier who risks his life in the belief that he is protecting himself and his family and community from some dire threat to their liberty and values. And the question that I wish to pose is how such conscientious self-sacrifice — not for family, nation or any in-group, but for mankind at large — can be defended in humanist terms as a rational or reasonable act. I am not asking whether humanists do in fact sacrifice their lives for such reasons of conscience more or less often than religious believers; or what the nature of their motivation is; but simply how their action is rationally defensible within the framework of humanistic belief. For the humanist would not, presumably, claim that such self-sacrifice is merely an irrational aberration; he would wish it to be seen as a consistent outcome of a distinctively humanist policy for living.

We need at this point to have before us a statement of the humanist ethic, and for this purpose I turn to Bertrand Russell's 'Human Society in Ethics and Politics'. (16) The major points of his theory are:

1. The notions of good and bad, or good and evil, arise from the fact that human beings are conscious of desires and aversions. If all experiences were equally welcome to us we should have no occasion to distinguish between them from the point of view of the desirability of their occurrence. But our nature is such that we seek some things (for example, pleasure) and shun others (for example, pain). 'I suggest', says Russell, 'that an occurrence is "good" when it satisfies desire, or, more precisely, that we may define "good" as "satisfaction of desire". One occurrence is "better" than another if it satisfies more desires or a more intense desire' (p. 55).

2. The ideas of right and wrong are dependent upon those of good and bad: "right" conduct is that which, on the evidence, is likely to produce the greatest balance of good over evil or the smallest balance of evil over good. . . . [The] sum-total of moral obligation is contained in the precept that a man ought to do right in the above sense' (p. 50).

3. Given that good is to be defined as satisfaction of desire, 'The general good will be the total satisfaction of desire, no matter by whom enjoyed. The good of a section of mankind will be the satisfaction of the desires of that section, and the good of an individual will be the satisfaction of the desires of that individual' (p. 60).

4. Our desires are not necessarily all self-centred. 'Most people desire the happiness of their children, many that of their friends, some that of their country, and a few that of all mankind' (p. 56).

5. Morality, central to which is the idea of an obligation to act rightly, has come about because we do not spontaneously seek the good of our group or of mankind as a whole. Ethics, in fact, is 'part of an attempt to make man more gregarious than nature made him' (p. 129). Thus, 'One may lay it down broadly that the whole subject of ethics arises from the

60

pressure of the community on the individual. Man is very imperfectly gregarious, and does not always instinctively feel the desires which are useful to his herd. The herd, being anxious that the individual should act in its interests, has invented various devices for causing the individual's interest to be in harmony with that of the herd. One of these is government, one is law and custom, and one is morality' (p. 124).

6. Russell recommends the ethical principle that the good which everyone ought to seek is the general good. 'When A says to B, "You ought to do X", I shall define the word "ought" as meaning that, of all acts that are possible for B, X is the one most likely to further the interests of mankind, or of all sentient beings' (p. 125). Consequently he can speak of 'the stock of all those mental goods which distinguish man from the ape and civilized man from the savage', and can say of them, 'It is these things that make the unique importance of man, and it is of these things that each generation in turn is the trustee. To hand on the treasure, not diminished, but increased, is our supreme duty to posterity' (p. 137).

To set this ethic within the context of the humanist conception of man's place in the universe I shall again quote Bertrand Russell. This humanist picture, which Russell eloquently articulated, depicts man as simply an intelligent and gregarious animal, destined to perish like the sheep and the grass, so that the moral and spiritual values which move him, and which form the basis of 'our supreme duty to posterity', have no status except as modifications of our consciousnesses, and are doomed to extinction with the extinction of these consciousnesses. As Russell wrote in a famous essay:

That Man is the product of causes which had no prevision of the end they were achieving; that his origin, his growth, his hopes and fears, are but the outcome of accidental collocations of atoms; that no fire, no heroism, no intensity of thought and feeling, can preserve an individual life beyond the grave; that all the labours of the ages, all the devotion, all the inspiration, all the noonday brightness of human genius, are destined to extinction in the vast death of the solar system, and that the whole temple of

Man's achievement must inevitably be buried beneath the débris of a universe in ruins — all these things, if not quite beyond dispute, are yet so nearly certain, that no philosophy which rejects them can hope to stand. Only within the scaffolding of these truths, only on the firm foundation of unyielding despair, can the soul's habitation henceforth be safely built. (17)

Russell's view then is that each individual automatically seeks his own good, which consists in the satisfaction of his desires; and that aspect of our nature which underlies the family and the propagation of the species leads many to include in the scope of their own good that of their spouse and of their offspring, at least when the latter are young and dependent. But the problem I am raising only comes into view when we consider the further extension of one's good far beyond this natural biological unit to the human species as a whole. For nothing less than this is required in the kind of case I have postulated, in which an individual voluntarily sacrifices his life for the sake of mankind. Let us now specify this case more fully by adding that his sacrifice is for the sake of future generations and that he has no offspring of his own through whom he might feel a more or less direct stake in the welfare of later generations. Such self-sacrifice for the good of mankind can only be the product of morality — of that device whereby the herd induces the individual to subordinate his own interests to those of the group. ('The herd, being anxious that the individual should act in its interests, has invented various devices for causing the individual's interest to be in harmony with that of the herd. One of these . . . is morality': 'Human Society in Ethics and Politics', p. 124.) The definition which Russell offers of the key moral notion of 'ought' or obligation, in terms of action in the interests of mankind as a whole, is thus itself simply a part of this device: in producing such a definition Russell is acting, whether consciously or not, as an instrument of the herd in disciplining its members.

Now let us grant that morality, as the psychological mechanism by which individuals are caused to serve their group, has its roots in the social side of man's nature. As Margaret Knight reminds us in a recent exposition of

62

humanist ethics, 'Animal psychology in recent years has undergone a minor revolution through the growth of ethology — the study of animal species in their natural state. One result of this development has been a growing realization of the extent to which gregarious animals exhibit co-operative, altruistic behaviour, not only towards sexual partners and offspring, but towards other members of what can reasonably be called the community.' (18) In the more gregarious of the lower forms of life, such as the ant, instinct plays the role played by morality in human life. The individual ant, we are told, fulfils his function automatically in the life of the ant-hill, even to the extent, if circumstances require it, of destroying himself for the preservation of the group. However, whereas the ant is moved to self-sacrifice by instinct, and so exercises no choice in the matter, man is able rationally to criticise the mechanism of conscience and to accept or reject its promptings. Imagine for a moment an ant suddenly endowed with the knowledge contained in Russell's book and with the freedom to make his own personal decisions. Suppose him to be called upon to immolate himself for the sake of the ant-hill. He feels the powerful pressure of instinct pushing him towards this self-destruction. But he asks himself why he should voluntarily embrace this fate. There is a cause that may lead him to do so, namely the force of instinct. But is there any *reason* why, having the freedom to choose, he should deliberately carry out the suicidal programme to which instinct prompts him? Why should he regard the future existence of a million million other ants as more important to him than his own continued existence? After all, they are all ants, all but fleeting moments of animation produced and then annihilated by mindless and meaningless forces — for that an ant 'is the product of causes which had no prevision of the end that they were achieving; that his origin, his growth, his hopes and fears, are but the outcome of accidental collocations of atoms . . .' is so nearly certain that it would be irrational to act on any other assumption. Since all that he is and has or ever can have is his own present existence, surely in so far as he is free from the domination of the blind force of instinct he will opt for life — his own life.

Now why should a humanist choose differently?

63

He experiences a tension between on the one hand the natural valuation of life by a living creature, so that he desires to continue to live, and on the other hand the claim of moral obligation, which presents itself to him as an absolute demand summoning him to sacrifice his life. For conscience characteristically takes the form of an unconditional claim upon us of such a kind that nothing else whatever, not even life itself, can legitimately outweigh it. Morality confronts our wills as, in Kant's phrase, a categorical imperative. And only such an absolute claim, against which nothing else can properly be set in the balance, could rationally lead one voluntarily to sacrifice one's life. Thus, in giving his life for purely ethical reasons anyone, whether humanist or religious believer, is implicitly acknowledging a moral claim upon him that is entitled to override even the basic natural desire for self-preservation. But in the case of a humanist this acknowledgement involves a profound self-contradiction. For he believes that morality is simply a device whereby the herd subordinates to its interests those of the individual. Thus from the point of view of his practice his official belief is false; and from the point of view of his belief his practice is irrational.

The irrationality arises from the fact that within the terms of the humanist philosophy it is unreasonable for anything to be of more value to a man than his own existence. For according to humanism we are simply complex animal organisms sustaining for some seven or eight decades an intermittent thread of consciousness. We have and are nothing but our own existence as consciousnesses subject to a series of agreeable and disagreeable modifications through time. To give this up is to give up everything, to be nothing, simply not to be. But we cannot rationally desire not to be so long as it is true for us that it is good to be alive. (19) On humanist principles no possible object of desire could, on a rational calculation, be worth to me the price of my own existence. There is nothing that can substitute for my own existence so as to give me either equal or greater satisfaction; for without my own existence nothing has the power to give me any satisfaction at all.

Let me put this point again slightly differently.

According to humanism there are simply individual

consciousnesses, who experience desires, and to whom anything that they desire but do not have, or have but would desire if they did not have it, is by definition good. That is to say, goodness is a correlate of either unfulfilled or fulfilled desire, and the attaining or retaining of the good, together with the avoidance of its opposite, comprises the motivation of human action. From the point of view of such a consciousness, his own existence is a necessary condition for anything being good to him and thus producing a motive for him to act. Now suppose that as a result of moral conditioning he finds that he desires there to be a state of affairs (the well-being of mankind in the future) which he can only help to bring about by prematurely ceasing to exist. He now has an object of desire the existence of which is incompatible with his own existence and thus with his having any desires. It is a good which he can desire to have but which in the nature of the case he cannot have. This paradox must provoke him to question whether he can rationally nurse such a desire. He can only conclude in the negative. For he cannot rationally take as an object of desire a state of affairs that would be incompatible not only with the gratification of any other of his desires but even with the gratification of this paradoxical desire itself. None of his desires can be satisfied if he no longer exists; and it cannot be the satisfaction of a reasonable desire of his that he should have no desires or their satisfactions. Therefore if he is able by the power of reason to discipline his emotions so as to reduce or eliminate this desire, he will certainly do so. It follows that the act of self-destruction for the sake of mankind is not an act that can be rationally chosen or defended within the limits of the humanist conception of man.

But might not our hypothetical humanist calculate that if he chose to preserve his own individual life at the expense of the future welfare of mankind he 'would be unable to live with himself' — he would be so tortured by remorse that life would not be worth having? And would not such a calculation provide a rational ground for his self-sacrifice? The answer, I think, is that it would not. For we are supposing the humanist to have 'seen through' the delusion of conscience; he knows that it is merely a device whereby the herd induces its individual members to subordinate their own

65

interests to it's. And having exposed this deception in his own mind he will no longer be subject to it. He will not feel any pangs of conscience after deciding to live out his own life rather than give it up for the sake of the herd.

But there is still another possible reasonable ground on which the humanist might make this sacrifice. (20) He might consider that the pleasure to be gained from contemplating the future good he is bringing about outweighs that to be derived from continued life. For it can be rational to prefer a briefer but more intense pleasure to a longer but less intense one. And if the humanist receives tremendous pleasure from the thought of the happiness of generations as yet unborn, he may feel amply compensated for the loss of another forty years of his own life by the enjoyment of this benevolent pleasure during the relatively short period prior to his self-sacrificial death.

There are however counters to this reasoning. One is that the period of time during which this pleasure is to be enjoyed might be very brief. It might be a matter of minutes or even only seconds. Is it then realistic to think of chosing a few seconds of pleasure, however intense, in preference to the prospect of some forty years of ordinarily enjoyable life? This seems a difficult question to determine: can the humanist be content to rely on a confident answer to it? We must also consider, as a limiting case, the act of mortal self-sacrifice for others which is an instantaneous response to some emergency, allowing no time at all between decision and act for the imaginative enjoyment of a future state of affairs, or indeed for the making of a hedonic calculus at all. Such a response would stem from the agent's existing basic moral stance or life-policy, which it would spontaneously embody in action in some moment of crisis. A humanist would, I think, want to be able without contradiction to admire and praise such a person. But if the argument of this chapter has been well founded it does not seem that he can.

Let me at this point emphasise again that I have not been discussing the psychological question whether a humanist would be likely to give his life for an ethical reason relating to the welfare of humanity as a whole; nor the comparative question whether a humanist is more or less likely to do this than a religious believer. I have been discussing the question whether such self-sacrifice on a humanist's part could be rationally defended on humanist principles. And the point that I have emphasised is that whilst we share with some lower animals social instincts which could, and indeed sometimes do, lead us to mortal self-sacrifice in the interests of the species, we also have a strongly developed individual self-consciousness and power of rational choice. And when we exercise this power within the framework of the humanist philosophy in a situation in which the social instinct summons us to such self-destruction, our reason can only see this urge as a deadly threat, to be resisted so far as possible. Thus in so far as the power of reason reigns in the lives of humanists they will never be guilty of the folly of ultimate self-sacrifice for the sake of the human community. And in so far as humanists think of such extreme self-sacrifice as praiseworthy, and as representing a pinnacle of human excellence, they are involved in a profound inconsistency.

The conclusion that I draw is of the same modest kind as in the cases of the design and cosmological arguments. We do not have here a proof of divine existence. But to follow out the implications of our own moral insights and convictions is to raise a question to which the answer *may* be — God. Is the mortal self-sacrifice for the good of humanity, which our moral nature prompts us to salute, rational or irrational? If the naturalistic picture of the universe is correct, such action is irrational and can occur only because men are not in the last resort able to assert their reason against the power of nurture, internalised as conscience. But if, on the other hand, we trust our conscience, believing it to be rational so to do, then we ought to disavow the naturalistic picture and move in a direction which might in the end lead to belief in God.

5 The Ontological Argument: First Form

(a) Introductory

The ontological argument is, philosophically, perhaps the most interesting of the traditional 'theistic proofs', involving as it does such fundamental concepts as perfection, deity, existence and necessity — both logical necessity and the idea of necessary being. It differs from all the other proofs in being *a priori*, proceeding from the idea of God as infinite perfection to his existence, instead of from some feature of the perceived universe to God as the ground either of its being or of its intelligibility. As an *a priori* argument it has the form of a logical demonstration; and as such it either totally succeeds or totally fails. It differs from the other arguments also in the scope of the conclusion which, if successful, it authorises. Whereas the other arguments profess to show that there is a divine designer behind the orderliness of nature, or a prime mover, first cause or necessary being behind finite existence — leaving open the question to what extent such a being possesses the moral attributes of deity — the ontological argument professes to demonstrate the reality of an unsurpassably perfect being. And it is more plausible, at least, to claim that such ideas as goodness, wisdom and love are contained within the notion of infinite perfection than that they are contained within the notion of a first cause or a necessary being. Indeed this was the ground of Kant's contention that the cosmological and teleological arguments both presuppose the ontological and cannot succeed if it fails: only the latter professes to link the idea of necessary and unconditioned reality with that of perfection. For given that the cosmological argument has shown that there is a necessary being, we can still ask what sort of a being this is. What reason have we for thinking it to be God, the infinite sum of perfections? Kant supplies a reason: 'The necessary being can be determined in one way only, that is, by one out of each possible pair of opposed predicates. It must therefore be *completely* determined through its own concept. Now there is only one possible concept which determines a thing completely *a priori*, namely, the concept of the *ens realissimum*. The concept of the *ens realissimum* is therefore the only concept through which a necessary being can be thought.' (1) But this reason uses the conclusion of the onto-logical argument: that the idea of a supreme being, or *ens realissimum*, necessarily entails the existence of such a being. Only if this conclusion is true can the cosmological argument amount to a proof of God's existence; but if that conclusion is true God's existence is already proved and the cosmological argument is entirely unnecessary. Thus the cosmological pre-supposes the ontological argument, and is rendered otiose by it. (2)

But whilst the ontological proof is thus the one which, if it succeeded, would succeed most definitively, and the one whose conclusion, if established, would be most worth establishing, it is also the one which, in the opinion of most philosophers, most definitively fails. Yet even in its failure it is still, from a philosophical point of view, in many ways the most rewarding of the proofs to study; and its fascination shows no sign of failing even after nearly a thousand years of intermittent discussion.

It will become clear as we proceed that the rather curious term 'the ontological argument' (3) names a family – though still a fairly closely knit familty – of arguments. And the founder of this famous family, despite certain previous stirrings of thought in a similar direction, was St Anselm.

Some writers have seen Anselm's reasoning prefigured in Augustine's 'De Libero Arbitrio', II, and have even regarded Augustine as the true originator of the ontological proof. Augustine's argument for divine existence does indeed approach Anselm's sufficiently closely for it to be altogether likely that it was the latter's reading of the 'De Libero Arbitrio' – in which, incidentally, the Fool who said, 'There is no God' is used to introduce the task of proving divine existence (II ii 5) – that first suggested to him the line of thought which he was to pursue so much further and more penetratingly than his master. (4)

A particular phrase that may well have passed directly into Anselm's mind, ultimately expanding into his new theistic argument, is Augustine's definition of God as that 'above which there is no superior'. (5) It is likely that this formula is a direct ancestor of Anselm's definition: 'that than which no greater can be conceived'. But nevertheless, Anselm's argument is not Augustine's: it is genuinely new, justifying the great excitement with which Anselm greeted it when it came to him in a flash of intellectual illumination comparable with the moment when the law of gravitation dawned upon Newton. (6) Augustine had argued in Platonic fashion that out intelligence must recognise something superior to itself, namely wisdom or truth; and either this is God, or, if there be something superior to it, then *this* is God. (7) Anselm's reasoning, however, as we must now proceed to see, was very different.

(b) Anselm's Proslogion 2 argument

Anselm (1033-1109), Abbot of Bec in Normandy and later Archbishop of Canterbury, was one of the most original and one of the most logically rigorous of Christian philosophical theologians. It was at Bec that in 1077-8 he wrote his 'Proslogion', a short work composed in the form of a prayer, in which he seeks in a single movement of thought to demonstrate both the existence and the nature of God; and it is here, and in Anselm's *Reply* to his first critic, Gaunilo, that his *a priori* argument for the existence of God is presented. It has recently been stressed that Anselm offers what can either be regarded as two arguments or two forms or stages of the same argument, the one in 'Proslogion' 2 and the other in 'Proslogion' 3 and the *Reply*. I do not think that Anselm himself regarded these as two different arguments; but nevertheless they have had widely different histories since his day and have in that sense *become* different arguments. The first argument (that in 'Proslogion' 2) was taken up by Descartes and criticised by Kant and has frequently been discussed in the histories of philosophy as 'the ontological argument', whilst the second has come into prominence only within the last decade or so, particularly through its advocacy, independently, by Charles Hartshorne and Norman Malcolm. I shall therefore discuss the two arguments separately before offering some thoughts about the relation between them.

Anselm formulates the concept of God in his famous definition: *aliquid quo nihil maius cogitari possit*, 'something than which nothing greater can be thought'. (8)

Even an atheist (represented by the biblical Fool who 'saith in his heart, There is no God') (9) can have this concept in his mind. Thus something-than-which-no-greater-can-be-thought exists *in intellectu* — as concept, or in the mind. The question is whether it exists not only in the mind but also in external reality (*in re*). The proof that it does is as follows. To exist in reality, as well as in the mind, is greater than to exist only in the mind. Therefore if something exists only in the mind it cannot be that than which no greater can be thought. For we can conceive of something greater than a 'greatest conceivable being' which exists only in the mind, namely that same thing existing also in reality. Therefore that than which no greater can be thought cannot exist only in the mind but must exist in external reality as well.

There are several points here which require commentary.

1. It is clear that by 'greater' Anselm does not mean spatially larger (and indeed he does not think of God as occupying space at all) (10) but 'more perfect'. Indeed he sometimes uses *melius*, 'better', in place of *maius*, 'greater'. (11)

2. The formula 'that than which no more perfect can be conceived' is open-ended and not circumscribing. That is to say, it does not tell us what God, as that than which no more perfect can be conceived, is like. Thus Anselm insists later in the 'Proslogion' that 'not only are You that than which a greater cannot be thought, but you are also something greater than can be thought.' (12) Accordingly the formula operates negatively, forbidding us to identify as God any being such that it is conceivable for this being to be surpassed in value. (13) The idea of God, according to Anselm, is the idea of the *ne plus ultra* in the dimensions (combined by neoplatonism) of reality and value.

3. Although the formula 'that than which no greater can be conceived' is in itself formal, and does not tell us what particular qualities must belong to such a being, yet Anselm believed that the theologian can in fact to some extent describe the divine nature by listing those attributes which it

71

is better to have than to be without. 'What goodness, then, could be wanting to the supreme good, through which every good exists? Thus You are just, truthful, happy, and whatever it is better to be than not to be — for it is better to be just rather than unjust, and happy rather than unhappy.' (14) Indeed the unfolding of the nature of God from the *aliquid quo nihil maius* formula by means of an intuitive knowledge of those qualities which it is better to have than to lack represents the programme of the 'Proslogion' as a whole.

Anselm does not deal with the question, which others have since raised, whether the resulting conception is one that could be instantiated. The possible existence of the unlimited sum of perfections has been queried at two points. First, does not existence necessarily involve limitation; and would not unlimited being thus be indistinguishable from non-being? Is there not, then, a contradiction in the notion of an infinite existent? The answer usually given to this question is that God does not 'exist' in the sense in which finite realities exist, i.e. by being one entity among others. Rather, he is 'being itself'; or he has actuality in distinction from existence; or he *is*, but does not exist as an item within the universe. Second, are the various perfections attributed to God compatible with one another when all are multiplied to infinity? (15) Justice and mercy, for example, seem to be mutually limiting attributes. A certain degree of justice can coexist with a certain degree of mercy; but is unlimited justice compatible with unlimited mercy? There are other aspects of the Christian concept of God which raise similar problems, independently of those generated by multiplication to infinity: e.g. can God be perfect and self-sufficient and yet a creator; can he be eternal and yet an agent in time; can he be immutable and yet love his creatures and sympathise with them in their sufferings? This is not the place to treat the large subject of the concept of God and its philosophical coherence. (On this see the volume in this series on 'Concepts of Deity'.) We must be content here to conclude that Anselm's argument operates against what M. J. Charlesworth (16) calls the 'factual atheist', who accepts the issue of divine existence as a meaningful question, which he answers in the negative, in distinction from the 'logical atheist', who denies that the concept of God is a viable concept in relation to which the question of existence or instantiation can properly be discussed at all. (17)

4. Anselm assumes the principle that it is better to exist (*in re*) than not to do so. 'For', he says, 'if it [i.e. that than which a greater cannot be conceived] stands at least in relation to the understanding, it can be conceived to be also in reality, *and this is something greater*.' (18) But how, it might be asked, do we know that it is greater or more perfect to exist in reality than not to do so? Is not this an unsupported assumption of Anselm's argument? And is not a contrary assumption also possible — as for example in the Buddhist rejection of empirical existence as evil?

There is indeed at this point a presupposed background to Anselm's reasoning, namely the background of neoplatonism, which reached Anselm both directly from Augustine and also from an intellectual mileu much of which had continued unchanged through the six hundred years that separated Augustine and Anselm, and within which neoplatonism was an important element. The neoplatonic picture of the universe embodied the long-lived and influential equation of being with goodness. The divine One is both absolute being and absolute goodness, so that goodness and being are in their ultimate source identical. (This pregnant thought doubtless goes back to Plato's teaching that it is the Good itself which is the source both of being and of goodness in everything else). (19) And they are likewise identical in our finite world, which is an emanation of the One, an 'overflowing' of the divine nature. The ultimate One radiates outwards to produce the universe, which is thus an extension by attenuation of what at its source is both Being itself and the Good itself. Thus the descending levels of being embody descending forms of goodness, less and less adequately expressing the fullness of the creative Good, until they vanish together into the non-being which is equated with evil. (20) Christian thought, rejecting the idea of divine self-emanation in favour of that of creation *ex nihilo*, nevertheless (and perhaps inconsistently) retained the platonic idea of the convertibility of being and goodness. Thus 'more perfect' meant for Anselm, as for Augustine, 'more being-ful' or 'more real'. And within this framework of thought it is self-evident that it is good to have being, since to have being is *ipso facto* to have goodness.

Neoplatonism apart, the premise that it is greater or more perfect to exist in reality than to exist only in thought would seem to represent a necessary presupposition or prejudice of consciously existing beings. For we should presumably not remain voluntarily in existence if we did not in practice accept this premise. Thus whether or not there is any further sense in which this proposition may said to be true, it is one to which existing free beings will always subscribe. It therefore seems permissible for Anselm to employ it in his argument.

5. It is to be noted that Anselm's formula does not refer to the most perfect being that there is, but to the most perfect possible being. That 'the most perfect being that there is, exists' is tautologically true. But 'the most perfect being that there is' might or might not be God, i.e. worthy of man's worship. The formula would leave open the possibility that the most perfect existing being is, for example, a human being and that there is nothing superior in value to man. However Anselm's formula is significantly different: that than which no more perfect can be thought, or is conceivable.

6. In an interesting article in the special Supplement devoted to the ontological argument in 'Religious Studies', 1968, M. J. A. O'Connor raises the question what force, if any, the word 'thought' has in the formula 'that than which nothing greater can be thought' or 'conceived' (*cogitari*). Would the meaning of the phrase be different without it: 'that than which nothing greater can *be*'? O'Connor argues that the *cogitari* adds nothing, or at least nothing that Anselm wanted to add; for it if adds anything, 'it builds into the definition relation to human thought as essential to God's nature. (21) But in that case Anselm's definition would be unacceptable. 'It would not define a transcendent necessary being, but a *contingent* being whose existence would be contingent on the existence of human thought, or whose qualities could not transcend human conceptions — a being who could not be greater than the greatest we can conceive. The definition is only acceptable therefore, if we regard the final word "thought" as merely rhetorical, if we treat the formula as meaning simply "something-than-which-nothing-

greater-can-*be*" and the final word "thought" as strictly redundant.' (22)

The only effect of the final *cogitari* O'Connor suggests, has been to obscure the all-important distinction between (a) the existence in the mind of that-than-which-nothing-greater-can-be and (b) the existence in the mind of the-*idea*-of-that-than-which-nothing-greater-can-be. The failure to focus upon this distinction, according to O'Connor, has led both Anselm and many of his critics to assume that the Fool acknowledges the ontological statement that that-than-which-nothing-greater-can-be exists in the mind when in fact he only acknowledges the psychological statement that the-*idea*-of-that-than-which-nothing-greater-can-be exists in the mind. And whereas from the ontological statement we might be able to proceed to the ontological conclusion that God exists in reality as well as in the mind, from the psychological statement we can only proceed to the conceptual conclusion that the idea of God is the idea of an existing being.

This is an ingenious suggestion; but nevertheless I am not convinced that it is correct.

As regards the alleged misunderstanding concerning what the Fool acknowledges, Gaunilo — Anselm's first critic — did indeed make this mistake, and Anselm promptly corrected it. Gaunilo drew O'Connor's distinction in paragraph 2 of his 'On Behalf of the Fool', and assumed that Anselm's argument requires that God somehow exists in the mind and not merely that the *idea* of God exists in the mind. However Anselm ('Reply', 6) corrects him, pointing out that his own argument only requires as its starting-point that the *idea* of 'that than which nothing greater is conceivable' exists in the mind. It therefore seems that the mistake which O'Connor sees as pervading the history of the ontological argument was scotched very early on, and certainly did not affect Anselm's own reasoning.

Nor, I think, is the *cogitari* in Anselm's definition dispensable. For in the shortened formula 'that than which nothing greater can be' there is an ambiguity in the term 'can' (*posse*). Is this a factual or a logical 'can'? Are we speaking of a being than which there cannot *in fact* be anything greater, because of surrounding circumstances of some kind in virtue of which there is no 'room' for anything to exist beyond a certain degree of 'greatness'; or are we speaking of a being than which a greater is not conceivable, because not logically possible? I think it is clear that Anselm intends the latter. 'That than which no greater can be thought' means that than which no greater is conceivable, i.e. logically possible. And Anselm differentiates this idea from that of the greatest that is possible within a given context or structure of fact by his use of *cogitari*. The *cogitari* is thus essential to convey the full force of his definition of God.

7. We are concerned here with Anselm's argument from the point of view of philosophy rather than of the history of ideas, and are therefore interested in it as an attempted proof of the existence of the greatest conceivable being. It should however be said that there are many important historical questions concerning Anselm's arguments, and many different attempted answers. Did Anselm intend to offer a proof of God's existence that ought to convince any rational inquirer; or was he explicating the inner logic of faith; or was he concerned to produce a mystical experience of the divine presence? Did the neoplatonic background of his thought mean that for him there was no problem of moving from an idea to reality, because ideas were for him already aspects of reality? There is no space to pursue such questions here; but a considerable amount of attention has been devoted to them, and the reader can find a brilliant conspectus of these investigations, together with valuable threads with which to find his own way through the extensive international literature, in A. C. McGill's 'Recent Discussions of Anselm's Argument'. (23)

(c) Gaunilo's criticism

The first critique of the 'Proslogion' proof came in Anselm's own lifetime in a short book entitled 'On Behalf of the Fool', presumed to be by Gaunilo, a monk of Marmoutiers; and Anselm's 'Reply' to this is quite as important as his original exposition in the 'Proslogion'.

Gaunilo's most important criticism is an attempted *reductio ad absurdum* by applying Anselm's reasoning to a most perfect island. The passage embodying 'Gaunilo's Island' is quite short and is worth quoting in full:

Consider this example: Certain people say that some-where in the ocean there is an island, which they call the 'Lost Island' because of the difficulty or, rather, the impossibility of finding what does not exist. They say that it is more abundantly filled with inestimable riches and delights than the Isles of the Blessed, and that although it has no owner or inhabitants, it excels all the lands that men inhabit taken together in the unceasing abundance of its fertility.

When someone tells me that there is such an island, I easily understand what is being said, for there is nothing difficult here. Suppose, however, as a consequence of this, that he then goes on to say: You cannot doubt that this island, more excellent than all lands, actually exists some-where in reality, because it undoubtedly stands in relation to your understanding. Since it is more excellent, not simply to stand in relation to the understanding, but to be in reality as well, therefore this island must necessarily be in reality. Otherwise, any other land that exists in reality would be more excellent than this island, and this island, which you understand to be the most excellent of all lands, would then not be the most excellent.

If, I repeat, someone should wish by this argument to demonstrate to me that this island truly exists and is no longer to be doubted, I would think he were joking; or, if I accepted the argument, I do not know whom I would regard as the greater fool, me for accepting it or him for supposing that he had proved the existence of this island with any kind of certainty. (24)

It will be noted that Gaunilo's definition of his island is not an accurate transposition of Anselm's definition of God. Instead of speaking of 'that island than which no more perfect can be conceived', Gaunilo speaks of an island 'more excellent than all lands' (*insulam illam terris omnibus praestantiorem*). This is an unfortunate formula. For it refers to that land — it does not matter whether it be an island or not — which is more excellent than all others. It merely speaks, in other words, of the most excellent land, in the sense of that land which is not excelled by any other. Gaunilo seems to think it impossible to prove that such a

77

land exists. But in fact nothing could be easier than to prove this, for it is a tautology that the most excellent land there is, exists. However (as we saw above, p. 74) this makes no connection with Anselm's own argument, which is not to the effect that the most excellent thing that there is, exists, but to the quite different effect that that than which no more excellent can be conceived exists.

However Gaunilo's formula has been tacitly rewritten by a succession of commentators so as to parallel Anselm's: an island than which no more perfect can be conceived. If one could use Anselm's own form of reasoning to prove the existence of such an island this would indeed be the *reductio ad absurdum* that Gaunilo was attempting. However Anselm denies that any such argument is capable of being formulated. 'I can confidently say,' he maintains, 'that if anyone discovers for me something existing in fact or at least in thought, other than "that than which a greater cannot be conceived", and is able to apply the logic of my argument to it, I shall find that "Lost Island" for him and shall give it to him as something which he will never lose again. (25) The point — developed in Anselm's 'Reply' as a whole and applied, though not very fully or explicitly, in paragraph 3 — is that 'that than which no greater can be conceived' exists necessarily, whilst an island (or any other finite object that Gaunilo might have chosen instead) can exist only contingently. Anselm's argument in its second form — and it is this second form that is developed in the 'Reply' to Gaunilo — is that it is more perfect to exist necessarily than to exist contingently, and that therefore that than which no more perfect can be conceived exists necessarily, and therefore exists. But this argument cannot be applied to 'that island than which no more perfect can be conceived.' An island, being by definition a part of the physical world and thus dependent for its formation and character upon other aspects of the world, as well as sharing the contingent nature of the world as a whole, cannot be the subject of the Anselmian argument. That reasoning only applies to the unique case of the being than which no more perfect can be conceived.

No discussions of Anselm's argument are known during more than a century following the appearance of the 'Proslogion'. But after this strange delay it received considerable attention in the thirteenth and fourteenth centuries, being attacked or defended (though not always in precisely Anselm's form) by Bonaventura, Thomas Aquinas, Duns Scotus and a number of others. But the second main period in the history of the ontological argument begins with René Descartes, the 'father of modern philosophy'. In his 'Meditations' (1641) he formulated a proof that is recognisably akin to Anselm's despite certain variations. (It is not clear whether Descartes had in fact read the 'Proslogion'; but if not he must surely have met the argument in some other writer's references to Anselm or in one of the forms in which the argument appeared in later medieval literature.) Descartes' definition of God differs from Anselm's. Instead of 'that than which no greater can be conceived' Descartes speaks of 'a supremely perfect being' (*un être souverainement parfait*). But his main contribution to the discussion of the argument consisted in highlighting the previously concealed assumption that existence is a quality or attribute or predicate such that it is possible to ask of a given *x* whether or not it has this attribute. Descartes asserts explicitly that 'existence is a perfection', (26) i.e. a desirable attribute, which it is more excellent to have than to lack; and he summarises his argument as that 'it is in truth necessary for me to assert that God exists after having presupposed that He possesses every sort of perfection, since existence is one of these.' (27)

Given, then, that existence is a perfection we can, Descartes claims, see an analytical connection between the other attributes of a supremely perfect being and the attribute of existing. He says:

It is certain that I no less find the idea of God, that is to say, the idea of a supremely perfect Being, in me, than that of any figure or number whatever it is; and I do not know any less clearly and distinctly that an [actual and] eternal existence pertains to this nature than I know that all that which I am able to demonstrate of some figure or number

79

truly pertains to the nature of this figure or number . . .
(28)

'Existence', he therefore concludes, 'can no more be separated from the essence [or definition] of God than can its having its three angles equal to two right angles be separated from the essence of a [rectilinear] triangle, or the idea of a mountain from the idea of a valley; and so there is not any less repugnance to our conceiving a God (that is, a being supremely perfect) to whom existing is lacking (that is to say, to whom a certain perfection is lacking), than to conceive of a mountain which has no valley.' (29)

The centrality, in Descartes' argument, of the concept of existence as a predicable characteristic is indicated again by his reply to an objection which he considers, namely that 'from the fact that I conceive of a mountain with a valley, it does not follow that there is such a mountain in the world; similarly although I conceive of God as possessing existence, it would seem that it does not follow that there is a God which exists.' (30) His reply is: 'from the fact that I cannot conceive a mountain without a valley, it does not follow that there is any mountain or any valley in existence . . . . While from the fact that I cannot conceive God without existence, it follows that existence is inseparable from Him, and hence that He really exists.' (31)

Ever since the logical structure of the argument was thus made clear by Descartes' work criticism has centred upon the premise that 'existence is a predicate', i.e. an attribute which something may have or lack. This assumption was challenged by one of Descartes' contemporaries, Pierre Gassendi, who declared that 'existence is a perfection neither in God nor in anything else; it is rather that in the absence of which there is no perfection.' (32) He continued:

This must be so if, indeed, that which does not exist has neither perfection nor imperfection, and that which exists and has various perfections, does not have its existence as a particular perfection and as one of the number of its perfections, but as that by means of which the thing itself equally with its perfections is in existence, and without which neither can it be said to possess perfections, nor can perfections be said to be possessed by it. Hence neither is existence held to exist in a thing in the way that perfections do, nor if the thing lacks existence is it said to be imperfect (or deprived of a perfection), so much as to be nothing. (33)

Descartes was unable to offer any reply beyond that of simply reaffirming the premise that had been challenged. (34)

Essentially the same criticism was later made, more influentially, by Immanuel Kant in his 'Critique of Pure Reason' (first edition 1781, second edition 1787). Kant's discussion is in two phases. (35) In the first he grants, hypothetically, the claim that the thought of the sum of perfection includes within itself the thought of existence, so that it would be self-contradictory to posit an all-perfect being (i.e. to suppose such to be) and yet to posit it as lacking existence. However, he insists, it by no means follows from this that there is an all-perfect being. Given the idea of an existing all-perfect being, the question remains completely open whether this idea answers to anything in reality:

If, in an identical proposition, I reject the predicate while retaining the subject, contradiction results; and I therefore say that the former belongs necessarily to the latter. But if we reject subject and predicate alike, there is no contradiction; for nothing is then left that can be contradicted. To posit a triangle, and yet to reject its three angles, is self-contradictory; but there is no contradiction in rejecting the triangle together with its three angles. The same holds true of the concept of an absolutely necessary being. If its existence is rejected, we reject the thing itself with all its predicates; and no question of contradiction can then arise. (36)

In the second phase of his discussion Kant challenges the concealed premise of the ontological argument that existence is a predicate which, like other predicates, can be included in the definition of a kind of object. 'Being unmarried' and 'having four feet' are examples of ordinary predicates which can figure in definitions; so that it is possible to demonstrate *a priori* that 'all bachelors are unmarried' and 'all quadrupeds are four-footed'. If existence were a predicate of the same logical type as these it would be possible to demonstrate *a priori*, as the ontological argument professes to do, that an all-perfect being has the attribute of existing. But against any such procedure Kant insists that '"*Being*" is obviously not a real predicate' and that 'all existential propositions [i.e. propositions of the form '*x* exists'] are synthetic.' (37) That is to say, the logical function of 'exists' is not to add a further predicate to a definition, but to assert that the definition applies to something in the world. In other words, 'By whatever and by however many predicates we may think a thing — even if we completely determine it — we do not make the least addition to the thing when we further declare that this thing *is*.' (38) Thus, 'The proposition, "God is omnipotent", contains two concepts, each of which has its object — God and omnipotence. The small word "is" adds no new predicate, but only serves to posit the predicate *in its relation* to the subject. If, now, we take the subject (God) with all its predicates (among which is omnipotence), and say "God is", or "There is a God", we attach no new predicate to the concept of God, but only posit the subject in itself with all its predicates, and indeed posit it as being an *object* that stands in relation to my *concept*.' (39)

The point has been made even more luminously clear in the twentieth century by the analysis of the function of 'exists' which is part of Bertrand Russell's theory of descriptions. (40) The upshot of Russell's discussions is that when we say for example, that 'cows exist' but that 'unicorns do not exist', we are not speaking about cows and saying of them that they have the attribute of existence, or of unicorns and affirming that they lack this same attribute. If that were the case we should have on our hands the problem of the status of those objects of discourse, such as unicorns, which are evidently in some sense 'there' to be talked about but of which we say that they do not exist. This problem has given rise to metaphysical theories which — if Russell is right — have been responses to a false problem.

We are talking instead about the *concepts* 'cow' and 'unicorn' and are saying of them that the one is instantiated and the other not. That cows exist means that the concept of a cow has instances; or putting it slightly differently, that the

82

propositional function '*x* is a cow' is sometimes true. And that unicorns do not exist means that the concept of a unicorn has no instances; or that the propositional function '*x* is a unicorn' is never true.

This account of the logical function of 'exists' is one of the few fairly generally agreed steps forward in philosophy; and its effect upon the ontological argument (in its first form) is to rule out its indispensable premise that existence is a predicable attribute. The issue of course is not whether 'exists' functions as a predicate in *any* sense, but whether it functions as the kind of predicate that the ontological argument requires it to be. Clearly 'exists' is grammatically a predicate. And beyond this it is possible to think of sentences in which it is natural to regard 'exists' as fulfilling the function of a real predicate — for example, 'This (apparent) table exists (i.e. is real rather than hallucinatory)', or 'This *x* exists (i.e. it is logically possible that it might not have existed)' (41); or again, 'President Nixon exists (i.e. is now alive), but President Kennedy does not'. (42) However these cases do not affect the conclusion that existence is not a predicate in any sense that would validate the ontological argument; for that argument does not seek to prove that God exists as a real in distinction from a hallucinatory material object, or as something presented that might not have been presented, or as a living in distinction from a deceased human being. The essence of the argument, in its 'Proslogion' 2 and Cartesian form, is that existence is a predicate such that it makes sense to say that a being which has it is superior to one which does not, and therefore that an unsurpassably perfect being must have it, and is thereby proved to exist. But existence is not a predicate in that sense, and any argument which presupposes that it is must be an invalid argument.

6 The Ontological Argument: Second Form

(a) 'Necessary being'

'Proslogion' 2 seems to be offered as an argument, complete in itself, for its conclusion that 'something than which a greater cannot be conceived undoubtedly both stands in relation to the understanding and exists in reality.' However 'Proslogion' 3 repeats the same form of argument, in terms now not of existence but of necessary existence — meaning by necessary existence (a phrase which Anselm himself does not use) the existence of something which is such that it cannot be thought not to exist. Anselm's argument in this second form is that it is greater to have necessary existence than not to have it; and that that than which no greater can be conceived accordingly has necessary existence and therefore necessarily exists.

'Necessary existence' or 'necessary being', as the existence of something which cannot be thought not to exist, can have at least three different meanings, and it is important to see what meaning it has in Anselm's argument.

1. It could be intended to mean logically necessary existence. For 'necessary' has come in philosophical discussion today to mean, primarily, 'logically necessary'. And there is prima facie support for the idea of logically necessary existence in the converse fact of logically necessary non-existence. For self-contradictory concepts are not merely contingently but necessarily not instantiated. Square circles and things that are both green and blue all over *necessarily* fail to exist: it is a logical truth that there are no such things. Why may there not, then, be a concept which is necessarily instantiated; an entity such that it is a logical truth that there is such a thing? And why may not the idea of the infinitely perfect being meet this specification?

The answer to this prima facie consideration is that the notions of necessary non-existence and necessary existence are not logically symmetrical. It is non-controversial that a

84

concept can guarantee its own non-instantiation by being self-contradictory. But the converse idea that a concept can guarantee its own instantiation, the idea in other words of a being whose existence is logically necessary, is excluded by the modern empiricist understanding of the nature of logical necessity.

In the first place, logical necessity is not a property of things but of propositions; so that 'logically necessary being' is, strictly, a meaningless conjunction of words. The proper question is not whether there is a logically necessary being, but whether the proposition 'God exists' or 'An unsurpassably perfect being exists' is a logically necessary truth. But if, as Hume, Kant, Russell and many others have argued, all existential propositions (i.e. propositions of the form 'x exists') are synthetic, then 'God exists' cannot, as an existential proposition, be logically necessary. Thus the notion of a being whose existence is logically necessary, or of whom it is a logical truth that he exists, is a malformed notion. A number of philosophers have assumed that the theologians' concept of God as necessary being is precisely this mistaken notion of God as *logically* necessary being, and have accordingly rejected the idea as meaningless. (1) But the concept which they are rejecting is not that employed by Anselm — or indeed by other major Christian theologians, such as Thomas Aquinas, who have spoken of God as necessary being.

2. It could mean that God's non-existence is unthinkable within the framework of theistic faith. This is necessity relative to a certain context, and is explained as follows by J. J. C. Smart, who introduced the notion into contemporary discussion:

It is not a *logical* necessity that the velocity of light in a vacuum should be constant. It would, however, upset physical theory considerably if we denied it. Similarly it is not a logical necessity that God exists. But it would clearly upset the structure of our religious attitudes in the most violent way if we denied it or even entertained the possibility of its falsehood. So if we say that it is a *physical* necessity that the velocity of light *in vacuo* should be constant — (deny it and prevailing physical theory would

85

have to be scrapped or at any rate drastically modified) — similarly we can say that it is a *religious* necessity that God exists. That is, we believe in the necessity of God's existence because we are Christians; we are not Christians because we believe in the necessity of God's existence. (2)

This is not however a concept of necessary being, but of necessary belief. Within the setting of Christian thought it is necessary to believe that God exists; and it is necessary in the sense that one who does not so believe is, by definition, not operating within the Christian thought-world. This necessity is thus relative to the acceptance of a systematic body of ideas which includes belief in the reality of God. This is not however at all what Anselm had in mind when he spoke of God as a being who cannot be thought not to exist.

3. Anselm himself states clearly what he means by a being which exists in such a way that it cannot be conceived not to exist. He says: 'that alone cannot be conceived not to be in which conceiving discovers neither beginning nor end nor combination of parts, and which it finds existing always and everywhere in its totality.' (3) He is here feeling towards what later became known as the notion of *aseity* (from *a se esse*) usually Englished as 'self-existence'. In its full development this is the idea of the existence of something that simply and unqualifiedly *is*, without beginning or end and without dependence for its existence or for its characteristics upon anything other than itself. If, following traditional usage, we describe such a being as 'necessary', this does not imply either a logically necessary being, or a being belief in whose existence is necessary within a certain conceptual framework. It describes instead what has sometimes been called a factually or ontologically necessary being.

From God's *aseity* his eternity, indestructibility and incorruptibility can be seen to follow. A self-existent being must be eternal, i.e. without temporal limitation. For if he had begun to exist or should cease to exist, he must have been caused to exist or to go out of existence by some power other than himself; and this would be inconsistent with his *aseity*. By the same token, he must be indestructible, for to say that he exists in total independence is to say that there is and could be no reality able to constitute or to destroy him;

86

and likewise he must be incorruptible, for otherwise his *aseity* would be qualified as regards its duration. Again, it is meaningless to say of the self-existent being that he might not have existed or that he merely happens to exist. For what would it mean to say of the eternal, uncreated Creator of everything other than himself that he merely happens to exist? When we assert of a dependent and temporally finite being, such as myself, that I only happen to exist, we mean that if such-and-such an event had occurred in the past, or if such-and-such another event had failed to occur, I should not now exist. But no such meaning can be given to the statement that a self-existent being only happens to exist, or might not have existed. There is no conceivable event such that if it had occured, or failed to occur, a self-existent being would not have existed; for the concept of *aseity* is precisely the exclusion of such dependence. There is and could be nothing that would have prevented a self-existent being from coming to exist, for it is meaningless even to speak of a self-existent being as *coming* to exist. (4)

We now have before us the two senses of 'necessary' which enter into discussions of the second form of the ontological argument — namely the logical necessity of analytic propositions and the factual necessity of eternal and independent beings — and can proceed to look at the argument itself.

(b) The argument in Anselm

Anselm's own discussion is concerned with ontological or factual necessity. He states his argument in slightly different ways in two successive paragraphs of 'Reply', 1. The first is as follows:

> If this [i.e. 'that than which a greater cannot be conceived'] can at least be conceived to be, it necessarily follows that it exists. For 'that than which a greater cannot be conceived' cannot be conceived to be, except as without a beginning. However, whatever can be conceived to be and actually is not can be conceived to be through a beginning. Therefore, it is not the case that 'that than which a greater cannot be conceived' can be conceived to

87

exist and yet does not exist. Therefore, if it can be conceived to be, it necessarily is. (McGill, p. 22.)

In examining this argument let us first identify the three concepts involved in it. They are:

A. The (one-member) class of that than which a greater cannot be conceived.
B. The class of things which can be conceived to be through a beginning.
C. The class of things which can be conceived to be and actually are not (i.e. which do not exist, but could possibly exist).

Anselm's argument, stated in a valid form, is:
Every A is a non-B
Every C is a B
∴ Every A is a non-C

The proper conclusion of the argument is thus that 'that than which a greater cannot be conceived' does not fall in the class of things which do not exist but could possibly exist. In other words, it is not the case that (a) the idea of God is the idea of a non-eternal or contingent being, and that (b) God, so defined, does not exist. It is not however hereby proved that he is a non-contingent being who does exist (or for that matter, though Anselm was not interested in proving this, that he is a contingent being who does exist). In short, it is not proved that God exists.

It may be useful to set forth this same argument of Anselm's again in a slightly different form, which I have used elsewhere: (5)

(i) To be unsurpassably perfect is to be incapable-of-having-a-beginning;
(ii) to be non-existent-but-capable-of-existing is not to be incapable-of-having-a-beginning; and
(iii) therefore to be unsurpassably perfect is not to be non-existent-but-capable-of-existing.

What this argument proves is that God is not non-existent-but-capable-of-existing, that is, that he is not

88

contingently non-existent. But it does not prove that he exists.

Anselm's second formulation is as follows:

> Further, if it can be conceived in any way at all, it is necessarily the case that it exists. For while someone may deny or doubt the existence of something than which a greater cannot be conceived, he will not deny or doubt that, if it does exist, then in fact and for the understanding it is impossible for it not to be. Otherwise, it would not be that than which a greater cannot be conceived. As for things which can be conceived and yet do not exist, even if such things were to exist, in fact and for the understanding it is possible for them not to be. Therefore, if 'that than which a greater cannot be conceived' can be conceived at all, it cannot not be. (McGill, pp. 25-6.)

Here the three concepts involved are:

A. The (one-member) class of that than which a greater cannot be conceived.

B. The class of things which can be conceived and yet do not exist (i.e. which do not exist, but could possibly exist).

C. The class of things such that it is impossible for them not to be.

Once again Anselm's own conclusion is a *non sequitur*, and the valid argument from his premises is as follows:

> All A's are C's
> All B's are non-C's
> ∴ All A's are non-B's

The conclusion is that 'that than which a greater cannot be conceived' does not fall in the class of things which do not exist but could possibly exist. That is to say, divine existence is not a contingent possibility which happens not to be realised. But in proving that 'that than which a greater cannot be conceived' is not a contingent which does not exist, it is not proved that it is a non-contingent which does exist.

To set out the valid part of Anselm's argument in another way: (6)

89

(i) Every non-existent-which-might-exist is a contingent;

(ii) no unsurpassably-perfect is a contingent;

(iii) therefore no unsurpassably-perfect is a non-existent-which-might-exist; and

(iv) therefore every unsurpassably-perfect is other than a non-existent-which-might-exist (i.e. is other than contingently non-existent).

Once again, what is proved is that God is not a contingent being, or more precisely that he does not contingently not-exist. In being other than a non-existent-which-might-exist he *either* exists *or* is a non-existent which could not exist (i.e. whose existence is impossible). But what is not proved is that he exists.

Having now examined, in the previous chapter, Anselm's 'Proslogion' 2 argument, and in this chapter his 'Proslogion' 3 and 'Reply' argument, we may next ask what the relation was in Anselm's own thinking between these two pieces of reasoning. And we may begin by noting that the distinction between them has been accentuated by the now traditional division of the 'Proslogion' into separate chapters, each with its own title — Chapter 2, 'That God Truly Is', and Chapter 3, 'That It Is Impossible to Conceive That God Is Not'. The original text formed a single continuous piece of prose with, for ease of reference, paragraph numbers in the margin and identificatory phrases attached to these numbers in a table of contents at the beginning. As A. C. McGill points out, 'It was not Anselm but his later editors who inserted the chapter titles into the text and so broke up its continuity into what look like self-contained and definitively entitled units. . . . For that reason, there are no grounds for *presuming* that Chapter II is a self-contained unit.' (7) Hence the question of the relation between the two forms or phases of Anselm's argument must be answered by reference to the internal logic of his reasoning rather than the external divisions of the text.

It appears to me that Karl Barth's view of the matter is essentially correct. (8) That is to say, Anselm is offering a single argument which divides into two phases. In the first phase he seeks to prove that God exists in the sense in which other things exist — that God is one of the items in a complete inventory of the universe. This is what Barth calls God's 'general' existence. But Anselm's overall concern in the 'Proslogion' is not simply to establish God's existence, but to establish in a single *argumentum* both his existence and his unique nature. And so in the second phase he seeks to show that the reasoning which proves God's existence also, at a deeper level, proves his unique nature as self-existent reality, as that which not merely exists but has necessary or ultimate existence. This is what Barth calls God's 'special' existence.

However the discussion of Anselm's intention is necessarily conjectural, and the philosophical consideration of the argument or arguments attributed to him does not depend upon the answer to such historical questions. Whatever Anselm's intention, it is still legitimate to emphasise the differences between the two phases of his reasoning and to argue, as Norman Malcolm and Charles Hartshorne have recently done, that whereas the argument in 'Proslogion' 2 is vulnerable to the Kantian criticism, that in 'Proslogion' 3 and the 'Reply' to Gaunilo is not.

(c) Norman Malcolm

In his important article 'Anselm's Ontological Arguments' (9) Norman Malcolm delineates with great clarity Anselm's concept of God's necessary being as eternal and independent existence. (10) He then quotes the first of the two paragraphs of Anselm's which I have discussed above (pp. 87-89), and comments:

> What Anselm has proved is that the notion of contingent existence or of contingent non-existence cannot have any application to God. His existence must either be logically necessary or logically impossible. The only intelligible way of rejecting Anselm's claim that God's existence is necessary is to maintain that the concept of God, as a being a greater than which cannot be conceived, is self-contradictory or nonsensical. Supposing that this is false, Anselm is right to deduce God's necessary existence from his characterisation of Him as a being greater than which cannot be conceived. (11)

91

Thus Malcolm's interpretation of the argument is as follows: An eternal being (12) either necessarily exists (in that by definition if he exists he cannot cease to exist) or necessarily does not exist (in that by definition if there is no such being, none can *come* to exist). Hence — to quote Malcolm's own words — 'God's existence is either impossible or necessary. It can be the former only if the concept of such a being is self-contradictory or in some way logically absurd. Assuming that this is not so, it follows that He necessarily exists.' (13)

This argument proceeds by ignoring the circumstances that the logical necessity and logical impossibility of God's existence are both, to use an anomalous phrase, hypothetical necessities: *if* God exists eternally, it is logically impossible for him, as an eternal being, to cease to exist; and *if* he does not exist, it is logically impossible for such a being to come into existence. In other words, it is logically impossible for the existence or non-existence, as the case may be, of an eternal being to be reversed. But one cannot deduce from this that providing the concept of an eternal being is not self-contradictory it is logically necessary that there is an eternal being. Even if the concept of an eternal being is entirely free from contradiction, it in no way follows that there must be such a being. For the 'logical necessity of God's existence' is simply the logical impossibility that, if he exists, he should cease existing. It is not logically impossible for there to be no eternal being, although it is logically impossible, *if* it is true that there is one, that it should become true that there is not.

However, later in his essay Malcolm discusses and seeks to rebut this view that the logical necessity of God's existence is a conditional necessity. He rejects the idea, first propounded by Caterus, a contemporary critic of Descartes, and then by Kant and subsequently by many others, that God's necessary existence means that *if* he exists, he exists necessarily. Malcolm's counter-argument is as follows:

I think that Caterus, Kant, and numerous other philosophers have been mistaken in supposing that the proposition 'God is a necessary being' (or 'God necessarily exists') is equivalent to the conditional proposition 'If God exists then He necessarily exists'. For how do they want the

92

antecedent clause 'If God exists' to be understood? Clearly they want it to imply that it is *possible* that God does *not* exist . . . . Let us make this implication explicit in the conditional proposition, so that it reads: 'If God exists (and it is possible that He does not) then He necessarily exists' . . . . But so far as from it being the case that the proposition 'God necessarily exists' entails the proposition 'It is possible that God does not exist', it is rather the case that they are *incompatible with one another!* Can anything be clearer than [that] the conjunction 'God necessarily exists but it is possible that He does not exist' is self-contradictory? Is it not just as plainly self-contradictory as the conjuction 'A square necessarily has four sides but it is possible for a square not to have four sides'? In short, this familiar criticism of the ontological argument is self-contradictory, because it accepts *both* of two incompatible propositions. (14)

But Malcolm is ignoring the circumstance that necessary being, in the case of God, is equivalent to eternal being (or, more fully, to *aseity*) and that the logical impossibility of an eternal being ceasing to exist is conditional upon an eternal being existing. We must therefore translate the absurd 'If God exists (and it is possible that He does not) then He necessarily exists' into 'If God exists (and it is possible that He does not) then He exists eternally'. (The corresponding proposition about a square would be 'If there is a square — and it is possible that there is not — then it necessarily has four sides'.)

(d) Charles Hartshorne

Charles Hartshorne has been maintaining the validity of the second ('Proslogion' 3 and 'Responsio') form of the ontological argument for a quarter of a century or more; and to him, more than to any other individual, must be given the credit for having evoked the current wave of renewed interest in the argument in the English-speaking world. Hartshorne's collection of writings on the subject, consisting of a book, several chapters in other books, and numerous articles, notes and rejoinders to reviews, (15) is so considerable that it has in the end diffused the impact of his contribution and made it harder, instead of easier, to concentrate upon his central contentions; and the highly polemical and almost obsessive tone of some of his writings on this subject has likewise tended to obscure their logical content. However in what is perhaps his most important essay on the ontological argument, 'Ten Ontological or Modal Proofs for God's Existence' in 'The Logic of Perfection', Hartshorne formalises his argument; and here we have a purely logical treatment which can be examined as such:

The logical structure of the Anselmian argument, in its mature or 'Second' form, may be partially formalized as follows:

q for $(\exists x)Px$, There is a perfect being, or perfection exists
N for 'it is necessary (logically true) that'
$\sim$ for 'it is not true that'
v for 'or'
$p \to q$ for 'p strictly implies q' or $N\sim(p \ \& \sim q)$

1. $q \to Nq$ 'Anselm's Principle': perfection could not exist [hence, the assertion that it exists could not be contingently but only necessarily true] (16)
2. $Nq \ v \sim Nq$ Excluded Middle
3. $\sim Nq \to N\sim Nq$ Form of Becker's Postulate: modal status is always necessary
4. $Nq \ v \ N\sim Nq$ Inference from (2,3)
5. $N\sim Nq \to N\sim q$ Inference from (1): the necessary falsity of the consequent implies that of the antecedent (Modal form of modus tollens)
6. $Nq \ v \ N\sim q$ Inference from (4,5)
7. $\sim N\sim q$ Intuitive postulate (or conclusion from other theistic arguments): perfection is not impossible
8. Nq Inference from (6,7)
9. $Nq \to q$ Modal axiom
10. q Inference from (8,9) (17)

I believe that this argument is fallacious. The fallacy is basically that already encountered in Malcolm and consists in an equivocation in the use of the term 'necessary'. Because

94

Hartshorne so conveniently formalises the argument one can point in his case to the exact place where this equivocation occurs, namely at prop. 6. The two senses of 'necessary' which are switched at that point are those discussed above: the logical necessity of analytic propositions, and the factual or ontological necessity of a being who is defined as having eternal and independent existence. Hartshorne himself states that his argument is to be understood exclusively in terms of logical necessity, which he defines in accordance with the modern empiricist doctrine that such necessity is ultimately tautological. Hartshorne says, 'In general it [N] means analytic or L-true, true by necessity of the meanings of the terms employed. This is the sense intended in the present essay.' (18)

However, if we interpret N in this way Hartshorne's argument fails decisively at the outset. For the first proposition reads:

'Perfection exists' strictly implies ' "Perfection exists" is logically true'.

In other words, Hartshorne's initial premise is that 'Perfection exists' is an analytic truth. But it is basic to the modern empiricist understanding of N, to which Hartshorne explicitily appeals, that existential propositions are *not* analytic and therefore not L—true. It is accordingly impossible to make sense of Hartshorne's first proposition in the terms in which he says it is to be understood. If his first proposition were acceptable, the argument could proceed by valid steps to its conclusion. But the initial proposition is ruled out by the very logic to which Hartshorne appeals when he says that N is to be interpreted as 'true by necessity of the meanings of the terms employed'.

To add to the difficulty, Hartshorne labels his first proposition 'Anselm's Principle', namely that perfection could not exist contingently. We have already seen that Anselm's principle is not that 'God exists' is an analytic proposition but that divine existence is eternal and independent existence ('that alone cannot be conceived not to be in which conceiving discovers neither beginning nor end nor combination of parts, and which it finds existing always and everywhere in its totality'). (19) It is clear from the texts that the notion of logical necessity in the modern sense was not in Anselm's mind; and it is therefore surprising that Hartshorne, who frequently chides the scholarly world for not bothering to read Anselm, (20) should so entirely have misstated Anselm's basic principle.

We are thus offered two conflicting clues. On the one hand Hartshorne's prop. 1 is to be interpreted in terms of the modern empiricist understanding of logical necessity as analytical; and on the other hand it is to be interpreted in terms of Anselm's notion of a factual necessity which is equivalent to *aseity*. The first interpretation, we have seen, is completely abortive. But the second, if we were to adopt it, would enable the argument to begin and to proceed as far as prop. 6:

1. That God exists means that he exists eternally.
2. Either God exists eternally or it is not the case that he exists eternally.
3. That God does not exist eternally means that it is eternally the case that he does not exist (eternally). (21)
4. Either God exists eternally or it is eternally the case that he does not exist (eternally).
5. That it is eternally the case that God does not exist (eternally) means that eternally he does not exist (eternally).
6. Either God exists eternally or it is eternally the case that he does not exist (eternally).

However if we thus interpret N consistently in terms of factual or ontological necessity, in accordance with Anselm's principle, the argument is unable to progress beyond this point. For from the disjunction in prop. 6 we cannot infer either that there is an eternal being or that there is not. We have proved that since the divine nature is defined as eternal, God's existence is either factually necessary (i.e. he eternally exists) or factually impossible (i.e. eternally he does not exist). But the argument does not supply us with any grounds for preferring one of these possibilities to the other.

In order that Hartshorne's argument shall proceed from prop. 6 to its conclusion in prop. 10, the meaning of 'necessary' has to change at this point from factual to logical necessity. Propositions 1-6 have to be interpreted in terms of factual necessity and 6-10 in terms of logical necessity, with prop. 6 itself being established as a conclusion in terms of the former and then used as a premise in terms of the latter.

With prop. 6 now understood as ' "God exists" is either logically true or logically false' (or 'God's existence is either logically necessary or logically impossible'), one can argue that 'God exists' would only be logically false if the concept of deity is internally incoherent, but that since it has not been shown to be so, we must assume the contrary. This assumption is Hartshorne's 'intuitive postulate' in prop. 7. (It will be remembered that Malcolm makes the same move: 'God's existence is either impossible or necessary. It can be the former only if the concept of such a being is self-contradictory or in some way logically absurd.') (22) The argument can then proceed:

6. Either 'God exists' is logically necessary or 'God does not exist' is logically necessary.
7. 'God does not exist' is not logically necessary.
8. 'God exists' is logically necessary.
9. ' "God exists" is logically necessary' implies 'God exists'.
10. God exists.

But the continuity of the argument from props. 1 to 10 depends upon the change of interpretation of N at prop. 6; and the argument as a whole is therefore irremediably invalid.

The conclusion of this whole discussion must therefore be that the second form of the ontological argument is after all subject to the same basic criticism as the first — it is unable to deduce real existence from a concept.

(e) A new Scotist modal argument

An American philosopher, James F. Ross, has recently published an interesting full-scale treatment of what can be described as a first cousin to Hartshorne's modal argument. Like Hartshorne, Ross argues from possibility to necessity; but whereas Hartshorne traces his own proof back to Anselm, Ross traces his to Duns Scotus. Ross's discussion is both lengthy and elaborate; but it leads eventually to two arguments which, he claims, 'adequately establish the existence of a being which is properly called "God" '. (23) The first argument is as follows:

1. It is possible that whatever is not the case should have either a self-explanation in terms of the inherent absurdity of its having been the case, or a hetero-explanation in terms of causes, agents, or producers whose actions prevent its being the case or whose own failure to act or to obtain is causally sufficient for its not being the case.
2. 'God does not exist' cannot be the case, because;
   (a) There is no absurdity or contradiction in 'God does exist', and hence 'God does not exist' is not self-explanatory.
   (b) 'God' cannot denote anything unless that thing be both uncaused and unprevented by any other thing and, furthermore, be both uncausable and unpreventable by any entity whatever. Therefore, 'God' cannot denote anything which is such that 'God does not exist' is hetero-explicable.
3. Then 'God exists' must be the case. (24)

This argument specifies two conditions under which it may be the case that x does not exist — (i) that the notion of x as existing is absurd or self-contradictory, and (ii) that something has causally prevented x from existing. But these are not claimed to exhaust the set of conditions under which it can be the case that x does not exist. ('It is *possible* [my italics] that whatever is not the case should have either . . . .') However the argument would only be formally valid if this list of two conditions were exhaustive. For the argument is that since neither of these two conditions applies to the non-existence of God, it cannot be the case that God does not exist, and therefore God does exist. But with the possibility left open that there may be other conditions under which it is the case that x does not exist, nothing at all follows concerning the existence of God — or indeed concerning the existence of anything.

If Ross were to seek to amend the argument by incorporating an assertion that his two conditions are jointly

98

exhaustive, we should be obliged to resist such a move. For Ross would thereby be begging the question. The whole issue is whether or not there could fail to be a God without the conception of God being defective and without there being any causes, agents or producers preventing there being a God. Let us agree that the concept of God is not self-contradictory. It does not follow that the existence or otherwise of God is a contingent matter, in the sense of being dependent upon causal factors. On the contrary (as Ross makes clear in 2(b)) the concept of God itself excludes this. If God exists he exists eternally and independently, and not as a result of causal conditions or permissions; and if there is no God, there is eternally no God, this situation likewise not being a result of any causal conditions. Only if God were defined as a finite object within the universe would his existence or non-existence depend upon causal circumstances. Thus Ross's first argument fails. His second argument is as follows:

1. That there is at least one Uncausable Producer [or uncreated creator] is logically possible.
2. Whatever is logically possible is either actual or potential.
3. Whatever is potential is causable.
4. No Uncausable Producer is causable.
5. Hence, no Uncausable Producer is potential.
6. Therefore, at least one Uncausable Producer is actual, that is, exists. (25)

A similar flaw appears in this argument. Is the meaning of 'logically possible' exhausted by the dichotomy 'either actual or potential' when this is glossed as meaning 'either actual or causable'? Clearly not; such a dichotomy only applies to contingent things. But the concept of God is the concept of an eternal and uncaused being. And whether or not there is such a being cannot be determined by a process of reasoning which applies only to contingents. Thus this argument also fails.

Having thus concluded that the ontological proof, in all its known forms, fails, we can nevertheless still ask whether, like the teleological, cosmological and moral arguments, it can

7 Rational Theistic Belief Without Proofs

(a) The religious rejection of the theistic arguments

We have seen that the major theistic arguments are all open to serious philosophical objections. Indeed we have in each case concluded, in agreement with the majority of contemporary philosophers, that these arguments fail to do what they profess to do. Neither those which undertake strictly to demonstrate the existence of an absolute Being, nor those which profess to show divine existence to be probable, are able to fulfil their promise. We have seen that it is impossible to demonstrate the reality of God by *a priori* reasoning, since such reasoning is confined to the realm of concepts; impossible to demonstrate it by *a posteriori* reasoning, since this would have to include a premise begging the very question at issue; and impossible to establish it as in a greater or lesser degree probable, since the notion of probability lacks any clear meaning in this context. A philosopher unacquainted with modern developments in theology might well assume that theologians would, *ex officio*, be supporters of the theistic proofs and would regard as a fatal blow this conclusion that there can be neither a strict demonstration of God's existence nor a valid probability argument for it. In fact however such an assumption would be true only of certain theological schools. It is true of the more traditional Roman Catholic theology, (1) of sections of conservative Protestantism, (2) and of most of those Protestant apologists who continue to work within the tradition of nineteenth-century idealism. (3) It has never been true, on the other hand, of Jewish religious thought; (4) and it is not true of that central stream of contemporary Protestant theology which has been influenced by the 'neo-orthodox' movement, the revival of Reformation studies and the 'existentialism' of Kierkegaard and his successors; or of the most significant contemporary Roman Catholic thinkers, who are on this issue (as on so many others) in advance of the official

101

teaching of the magisterium. Accordingly we have now to take note of this theological rejection of the theistic proofs, ranging from a complete lack of concern for them to a positive repudiation of them as being religiously irrelevant or even harmful. There are several different considerations to be evaluated.

1. It has often been pointed out that for the man of faith, as he is depicted in the Bible, no theistic proofs are necessary. (5) Philosophers in the rationalist tradition, holding that to know means to be able to prove, have been shocked to find that in the Bible, which is supposed to be the basis of Western religion, no attempt whatever is made to demonstrate the existence of God. Instead of professing to establish the divine reality by philosophical reasoning the Bible throughout takes this for granted. Indeed to the biblical writers it would have seemed absurd to try to establish by logical argumentation that God exists. For they were convinced that they were already having to do with him and he with them in all the affairs of their lives. They did not think of God as an inferred entity but as an experienced reality. Many of the biblical writers were (sometimes, though doubtless not at all times) as vividly conscious of being in God's presence as they were of living in a material world. It is impossible to read their pages without realising that to them God was not a proposition completing a syllogism, or an idea adopted by the mind, but the supreme experiential reality. It would be as sensible for a husband to desire a philosophical proof of the existence of the wife and family who contribute so much of the meaning and value of his life as for the man of faith to seek for a proof of the existence of the God within whose purpose he believes that he lives and moves and has his being.

As Cook Wilson wrote:

If we think of the existence of our friends; it is the 'direct knowledge' which we want: merely inferential knowledge seems a poor affair. To most men it would be as surprising as unwelcome to hear it could not be directly known whether there were such existences as their friends, and that it was only a matter of (probable) empirical argument and inference from facts which are directly known. And
102

even if we convince ourselves on reflection that this is really the case, our actions prove that we have a confidence in the existence of our friends which can't be derived from an empirical argument (which can never be certain) for a man will risk his life for his friend. We don't want merely inferred friends. Could we possibly be satisfied with an inferred God? (6)

In other words the man of faith has no need of theistic proofs; for he has something which for him is much better. However it does not follow from this that there may not be others who do need a theistic proof, nor does it follow that there are in fact no such proofs. All that has been said about the irrelevance of proofs to the life of faith may well be true, and yet it might still be the case that there are valid arguments capable of establishing the existence of God to those who stand outside the life of faith.

2. It has also often been pointed out that the God whose existence each of the traditional theistic proofs professes to establish is only an abstraction from and a pale shadow of the living God who is the putative object of biblical faith. A First Cause of the Universe might or might not be a deity to whom an unqualified devotion, love and trust would be appropriate; Aquinas's *Et hoc omnes intelligunt Deum* ('and this all understand to be God') is not the last step in a logical argument but merely an exercise of the custom of overlooking a gap in the argument at this point. A Necessary Being, and indeed a being who is metaphysically absolute in every respect — omnipotent, omniscient, eternal, uncreated — might be morally good or evil. As H. D. Aitken has remarked, 'Logically, there is no reason why an almighty and omniscient being might not be a perfect stinker. (7) A divine Designer of the world whose nature is read off from the appearances of nature might, as Hume showed, be finite or infinite, perfect or imperfect, omniscient or fallible, and might indeed be not one being but a veritable pantheon. (8) It is only by going beyond what is proved, or claimed to have been proved, and identifying the First Cause, Necessary Being, or Mind behind Nature with the God of biblical faith that these proofs could ever properly impel to worship. By themselves and without supplementation of content and

infusion of emotional life from religious traditions and experiences transcending the proofs themselves they would never lead to the life of faith.

The ontological argument on the other hand is in this respect in a different category. If it succeeds it establishes the reality of a being so perfect in every way that no more perfect can be conceived. Clearly if such a being is not worthy of worship none ever could be. It would therefore seem that, unlike the other proofs, the ontological argument, if it were logically sound, would present the relatively few persons who are capable of appreciating such abstract reasoning with a rational ground for worship. On the other hand, however, whilst this is the argument that would accomplish most if it succeeded it is also the argument which is most absolutely incapable of succeeding; for it is, as we have seen, inextricably involved in the fallacy of professing to deduce existence from a concept.

3. It is argued by some religious writers that a logical demonstration of the existence of God would be a form of coercion and would as such be incompatible with God's evident intention to treat his human creatures as free and responsible persons. A great deal of twentieth-century theology emphasises that God as the infinite personal reality, having made man as person in his own image, always treats men as persons, respecting their relative freedom and autonomy. He does not override the human mind by revealing himself in overwhelming majesty and power, but always approaches us in ways that leave room for an un-compelled response of human faith. Even God's own entry into our earthly history, it is said, was in an 'incognito' that could be penetrated only by the eyes of faith. As Pascal put it, 'willing to appear openly to those who seek him with all their heart, and to be hidden from those who flee from him with all their heart, he so regulates the knowledge of himself that he has given indications of himself which are visible to those who seek him and not to those who do not seek him. There is enough light for those to see who only desire to see, and enough obscurity for those who have a contrary disposition.' (9) God's self-revealing actions are accordingly always so mediated through the events of our temporal experience that men only become aware of the divine

104

presence by interpreting and responding to these events in the way which we call religious faith. For if God were to disclose himself to us in the coercive manner in which our physical environment obtrudes itself we should be dwarfed to nothingness by the infinite power thus irresistibly breaking open the privacy of our souls. Further, we should be spiritually blinded by God's perfect holiness and paralysed by his infinite energy; 'for human kind cannot bear very much reality.' (10) Such a direct, unmediated confrontation breaking in upon us and shattering the frail autonomy of our finite nature would leave no ground for a free human response of trust, self-commitment and obedience. There could be no call for a man to venture upon a dawning consciousness of God's reality and thus to receive this consciousness as an authentic part of his own personal existence precisely because it has not been injected into him or clamped upon him by magisterial exercise of divine omnipotence.

The basic principle invoked here is that for the sake of creating a personal relationship of love and trust with his human creatures God does not force an awareness of himself upon them. And (according to the view which we are considering) it is only a further application of the same principle to add that a logically compelling demonstration of God's existence would likewise frustrate this purpose. For men — or at least those of them who are capable of following the proof — could then be forced to know that God is real. Thus Alasdair MacIntyre, when a Christian apologist, wrote: 'For if we could produce logically cogent arguments we should produce the kind of certitude that leaves no room for decision; where proof is in place, decision is not. We do not decide to accept Euclid's conclusions; we merely look to the rigour of his arguments. If the existence of God were demonstrable we should be as bereft of the possibility of making a free decision to love God as we should be if every utterance of doubt or unbelief was answered by thunderbolts from heaven.' (11) This is the 'religious coercion' objection to the theistic proofs.

To what extent is it a sound objection? We may accept the theological doctrine that for God to force men to know him by the coercion of logic would be incompatible with his purpose of winning the voluntary response and worship of

105

free moral beings. But the question still remains whether the theistic proofs could ever do this. Could a verbal proof of divine existence compel a consciousness of God comparable in coerciveness with a direct manifestation of his divine majesty and power? Could anyone be moved and shaken in their whole being by the demonstration of a proposition, as men have been by a numinous experience of overpowering impressiveness? Would the things that have just been said about an overwhelming display of divine glory really apply to verbal demonstrations — that infinite power would be irresistibly breaking in upon the privacy of our souls and that we should be blinded by God's perfect holiness and paralysed by his infinite energy? Indeed could a form of words, culminating in the proposition that 'God exists', ever have power by itself to produce more than what Newman calls a notional assent in our minds? (12)

It is of course true that the effect of purely rational considerations such as those which are brought to bear in the theistic proofs are much greater in some minds than in others. The more rational the mind the more considerable is the effect to be expected. In many persons — indeed taking mankind as a whole, in the great majority — the effect of a theistic proof, even when no logical flaw is found in it, would be virtually nil! But in more sophisticated minds the effect must be greater, and it is at least theoretically possible that there are minds so rational that purely logical considerations can move them as effectively as the evidence of their senses. It is therefore conceivable that someone who is initially agnostic might be presented with a philosophical proof of divine existence — say the ontological argument, with its definition of God as that than which no more perfect can be conceived — and might as a result be led to worship the being whose reality has thus been demonstrated to him. This seems to be possible; but I believe that even in such a case there must, in addition to an intelligent appreciation of the argument, be a distinctively religious response to the idea of God which the argument presents. Some propensity to respond to unlimited perfection as holy and as rightly claiming a response of unqualified worship and devotion must operate, over and above the purely intellectual capacity for logical calculation. (13) For we can conceive of a purely

106

or merely logical mind, a kind of human calculating machine, which is at the same time devoid of the capacity for numinous feeling and worshipping response. Such a being might infer that God exists but be no more existentially interested in this conclusion than many people are in, say, the fact that the Shasta Dam is 602 feet high. It therefore seems that when the acceptance of a theistic proof leads to worship, a religious reaction occurs which turns what would otherwise be a purely abstract conclusion into an immensely significant and moving fact. In Newman's terminology, when a notional assent to the proposition that God exists becomes a real assent, equivalent to an actual living belief and faith in God, there has been a free human response to an idea which could instead have been rejected by being held at the notional level. In other words, a verbal proof of God's existence cannot by itself break down our human freedom; it can only lead to a notional assent which has little or no positive religious value or substance.

I conclude, then, that the theological objections to the theistic proofs are considerably less strong than the philosophical ones; and that theologians who reject natural theology would therefore do well to do so primarily on philosophical rather than on theological grounds. These philosophical reasons are, as we have seen, very strong; and we therefore now have to consider whether, in the absence of any theistic proofs, it can nevertheless be rational to believe in the existence of God.

(b) Can there be rational theistic belief without proofs?

During the period dominated by the traditional theistic arguments the existence of God was often treated by philosophers as something to be discovered through reasoning. It was seen as the conclusion of an inference; and the question of the rationality of the belief was equated with that of the soundness of the inference. But from a religious point of view, as we have already seen, there has always been something very odd about this approach. The situation which it envisages is that of people standing outside the realm of faith, for whom the apologist is trying to build a bridge of rational inference to carry them over the frontier into that realm. But of course this is not the way in which religious faith has originally or typically or normally come about. When the cosmological, ontological, teleological and moral arguments were developed, theistic belief was already a functioning part of an immemorially established and developing form of human life. The claims of religion are claims made by individuals and communities on the basis of their experience — and experience which is none the less their own for occuring within an inherited framework of ideas. We are not dealing with a merely conceivable metaphysical hypothesis which someone has speculatively invented but which hardly anyone seriously believes. We are concerned, rather, with convictions born out of experience and reflection and living within actual communities of faith and practice. Historically, then, the philosophical 'proofs' of God have normally entered in to support and confirm but not to create belief. Accordingly the proper philosophical approach would seem to be a probing of the actual foundations and structure of a living and operative belief rather than of theoretical and non-operative arguments subsequently formulated for holding those beliefs. The question is not whether it is possible to prove, starting from zero, that God exists; the question is whether the religious man, given the distinctively religious form of human existence in which he participates, is properly entitled as a rational person to believe what he does believe?

At this point we must consider what we mean by a rational belief. If by a belief we mean a proposition believed, then what we are to be concerned with here are not rational beliefs but rational believings. Propositions can be well-formed or ill-formed, and they can be true or false, but they cannot be rational or irrational. It is *people* who are rational or irrational, and derivately their states and their actions, including their acts and states of believing. Further, apart from the believing of analytic propositions, which are true by definition and are therefore rationally believed by anyone who understands them, the rationality of acts (or states) of believing has to be assessed separately in each case. For it is a function of the relation between the proposition believed and the evidence on the basis of which the believer believes it. It might conceivably be rational for Mr X to believe p but not

108

rational for Mr Y to believe p, because in relation to the data available to Mr X p is worthy of belief but not in relation to the date available to Mr Y. Thus the question of the rationality of belief in the reality of God is the question of the rationality of a particular person's believing, given the data that he is using; or that of the believing of a class of people who share the same body of data. Or putting the same point the other way round, any assessing of the belief-worthiness of the proposition that God exists must be an assessing of it in relation to particular ranges of data.

Now there is one area of data or evidence which is normally available to those who believe in God, and that provides a very important part of the ground of their believing, but which is normally not available to and therefore not taken into account by those who do not so believe; and this is religious experience. It seems that the religious man is in part basing his believing upon certain data of religious experience which the non-religious man is not using because he does not have them. Thus our question resolves itself into one about the theist's right, given his distinctively religious experience, to be certain that God exists. It is the question of the rationality or irrationality, the well-groundedness or ill-groundedness, of the religious man's claim to know God. The theist cannot hope to prove that God exists; but despite this it may nevertheless be possible for him to show it to be wholly reasonable for him to believe that God exists.

What is at issue here is not whether it is rational for some-one else, who does not participate in the distinctively religious mode of experience, to believe in God on the basis of the religious man's reports. I am not proposing any kind of 'argument from religious experience' by which God is inferred as the cause of the special experiences described by mystics and other religious persons. It is not the non-religious man's theoretical use of someone else's reported religious experience that is to be considered, but the religious man's own practical use of it. The question is whether he is acting rationally in trusting his own experience and in proceeding to live on the basis of it.

In order to investigate this question we must consider what counts as rational belief in an analogous case. The analogy

109

that I propose is that between the religious person's claim to be conscious of God and any man's claim to be conscious of the physical world as an environment, existing independently of himself, of which he must take account.

In each instance a realm of putatively cognitive experience is taken to be veridical and is acted upon as such, even though its veridical character cannot be logically demonstrated. So far as sense experience is concerned this has emerged both from the failure of Descartes' attempt to provide a theoretical guarantee that our senses relate us to a real material environment, and from the success of Hume's attempt to show that our normal non-solipsist belief in an objective world of enduring objects around us in space is neither a product of, nor justifiable by, philosophical reasoning but is what has been called in some expositions of Hume's thought (though the term does not seem to have been used by Hume himself) a natural belief. It is a belief which naturally and indeed inevitably arises in the normal human mind in response to normal human perceptual experience. It is a belief on the basis of which we live and the rejection of which, in favour of a serious adoption of the solipsist alternative, would so disorient our relationship to other persons within a common material environment that we should be accounted insane. Our insanity would consist in the fact that we should no longer regard other people as independent centres of consciousness, with their own purposes and wills, with whom interpersonal relationships are possible. We should instead be living in a one-person world.

It is thus a basic truth in, or a presupposition of, our language that it is rational or sane to believe in the reality of the external world that we inhabit in common with other people, and irrational or insane not to do so.

What are the features of our sense experience in virtue of which we all take this view? They would seem to be twofold: the givenness or the involuntary character of this form of cognitive experience, and the fact that we can and do act successfully in terms of our belief in an external world. That is to say, being built and circumstanced as we are we cannot help initially believing as we do, and our belief is not contradicted, but on the contrary continuously confirmed, by our continuing experience. These characteristics jointly

110

constitute a sufficient reason to trust and live on the basis of our perceptual experience in the absence of any positive reason to distrust it; and our inability to exclude the theoretical possibility of our experience as a whole being purely subjective does not constitute such a reason. This seems to be the principle on which, implicitly, we proceed. And it is, by definition, rational to proceed in this way. That is to say, this is the way in which all human beings do proceed and have proceeded, apart from a very small minority who have for that very reason been labelled by the majority as insane. This habitual acceptance of our perceptual experience is thus, we may say, part of our operative concept of human rationality.

We can therefore now ask whether a like principle may be invoked on behalf of a parallel response to religious experience. 'Religious experience' is of course a highly elastic concept. Let us restrict attention, for our present purpose, to the theistic 'sense of the presence of God', the putative awareness of a transcendent divine Mind within whose field of consciousness we exist and with whom therefore we stand in a relationship of mutual awareness. This sense of 'living in the divine presence' does not take the form of a direct vision of God, but of experiencing events in history and in our own personal life as the medium of God's dealings with us. Thus religious differs from non-religious experience, not as the awareness of a different world, but as a different way of experiencing the same world. Events which can be experienced as having a purely natural significance are experienced by the religious mind as having also and at the same time religious significance and as mediating the presence and activity of God. (14)

It is possible to study this type of religious experience either in its strongest instances, in the primary and seminal religious figures, or in its much weaker instances in ordinary adherents of the traditions originated by the great exemplars of faith. Since we are interested in the question of the claims which religious experience justifies it is appropriate to look at that experience in its strongest and purest forms. A description of this will accordingly apply only very partially to the ordinary rank-and-file believer either of today or in the past.

111

If then we consider the sense of living in the divine presence as this was expressed by, for example, Jesus of Nazareth, or by St Paul, St Francis, St Anselm or the great prophets of the Old Testament, we find that their 'awareness of God' was so vivid that he was as indubitable a factor in their experience as was their physical environment. They could no more help believing in the reality of God than in the reality of the material world and of their human neighbours. Many of the pages of the Bible resound with the sense of God's presence as a building might reverberate from the tread of some gigantic being walking through it. God was known to the prophets and apostles as a dynamic will interacting with their own wills; a sheerly given personal reality, as inescapably to be reckoned with as destructive storm and life-giving sunshine, the fixed contours of the land, or the hatred of their enemies and the friendship of their neighbours.

Our question concerns, then, one whose 'experience of God' has this compelling quality, so that he is no more inclined to doubt its veridical character than to doubt the evidence of his senses. Is it rational for him to take the former, as it is certainly rational for him to take the latter, as reliably cognitive of an aspect of his total environment and thus as knowledge in terms of which to act? Are the two features noted above in our sense experience — its givenness, or involuntary character, and the fact that we can successfully act in terms of it — also found here? It seems that they are. The sense of the presence of God reported by the great religious figures has a similar involuntary and compelling quality; and as they proceed to live on the basis of it they are sustained and confirmed by their further experiences in the conviction that they are living in relation, not to illusion, but to reality. It therefore seems prima facie, that the religious man *is* entitled to trust his religious experience and to proceed to conduct his life in terms of it.

The analogy operating within this argument is between our normal acceptance of our sense experience as perception of an objective external world, and a corresponding acceptance of the religious experience of 'living in God's presence' as the awareness of a divine reality external to our own minds. In each case there is a solipsist alternative in which one can

112

affirm *solus ipse* to the exclusion of the transcendent — in the one case denying a physical environment transcending our own private consciousness and in the other case denying a divine Mind transcending our own private consciousness. It should be noted that this analogy is not grounded in the perception of particular material objects and does not turn upon the contrast between veridical and illusory sense perceptions, but is grounded in our awareness of an objective external world as such and turns upon the contrast between this and a theoretically possible solipsist interpretation of the same stream of conscious experience.

(c) Religious and perceptual belief

Having thus set forth the analogy fairly boldly and starkly I now want to qualify it by exploring various differences between religious and sensory experience. The resulting picture will be more complex than the first rough outline presented so far; and yet its force as supporting the rationality of theistic faith will not, I think, in the end have been undermined.

The most obvious difference is that everyone has and cannot help having sense experiences, whereas not everyone has religious experiences, at any rate of the very vivid and distinct kind to which we have been referring. As bodily beings existing in a material environment, we cannot help interacting consciously with that environment. That is to say, we cannot help 'having' a stream of sense experiences; and we cannot help accepting this as the perception of a material world around us in space. When we open our eyes in daylight we cannot but receive the visual experiences that come to us; and likewise with the other senses. And the world which we thus perceive is not plastic to our wishes but presents itself to us as it is, whether we like it or not. Needless to say, our senses do not coerce us in any sense of the word 'coerce' that implies unwillingness on our part, as when a policeman coerces an unwilling suspect to accompany him to the police station. Sense experience is coercive in the sense that we cannot when sane believe that our material environment is not broadly as we perceive it to be, and that if we did momentarily persuade ourselves that what we experience is not there we should quickly be penalised by the environment and indeed, if we persisted, destroy by it. (15)

In contrast to this we are not obliged to interact consciously with a spiritual environment. Indeed it is a commonplace of much contemporary theology that God does not force an awareness of himself upon mankind but leaves us free to know him by an uncompelled response of faith. And yet once a man has allowed himself freely to become conscious of God — it is important to note — that experience is, at its top levels of intensity, coercive. It creates the situation of the person who *cannot help* believing in the reality of God. The apostle, prophet or saint may be so vividly aware of God that he can no more doubt the veracity of his religious awareness than of his sense experience. During the periods when he is living consciously in the presence of God, when God is to him the divine Thou, the question whether God exists simply does not arise. Our cognitive freedom in relation to God is not to be found at this point but at the prior stage of our coming to be aware of him. The individual's own free receptivity and responsiveness plays an essential part in his dawning consciousness of God; but once he *has* become conscious of God that consciousness can possess a coercive and indubitable quality. (16)

It is a consequence of this situation that whereas everyone perceives and cannot help perceiving the physical world, by no means everyone experiences the presence of God. Indeed only rather few people experience religiously in the vivid and coercive way reported by the great biblical figures. And this fact immediately suggests a sceptical question. Since those who enjoy a compelling religious experience form such a small minority of mankind, ought we not to suspect that they are suffering from a delusion comparable with that of the paranoiac who hears threatening voices from the walls or the alcoholic who sees green snakes?

This is of course a possible judgement to make. But this judgement should not be made *a priori*, in the absence of specific grounds such as we have in the other cases mentioned. And it would in fact be difficult to point to adequate evidence to support this hypothesis. On the contrary the general intelligence and exceptionally high moral quality of the great religious figures clashes with any analysis of their experience in terms of abnormal psychology. Such analyses are not indicated, as is the parallel view of paranoiacs and alcoholics, by evidence of general disorientation to reality or of incapacity to live a productive and satisfying life. On the contrary, Jesus of Nazareth, for example, has been regarded by hundreds of millions of people as the fulfilment of the ideal possibilities of human nature. A more reasonable negative position would therefore seem to be the agnostic one that whilst it is proper for the religious man himself, given his distinctive mode of experience, to believe firmly in the reality of God, one does not oneself share that experience and therefore has no ground upon which to hold that belief. Theism is then not positively denied, but is on the other hand consciously and deliberately not affirmed. This agnostic position must be accepted by the theist as a proper one. For if it is reasonable for one man, on the basis of his distinctively religious experience, to affirm the reality of God it must also be reasonable for another man, in the absence of any such experience, not to affirm the reality of God.

The next question that must be raised is the closely connected one of the relation between rational belief and truth. I suggested earlier that, strictly, one should speak of rational believings rather than of rational beliefs. But nevertheless it is sometimes convenient to use the latter phrase, which we may then understand as follows. By a rational belief we shall mean a belief which it is rational for the one who holds it to hold, given he data available to him. Clearly such beliefs are not necessarily or always true. It is sometimes rational for an individual to have, on the basis of incomplete data, a belief which is in fact false. For example, it was once rational for people to believe that the sun revolves round the earth; for it was apparently perceived to do so, and the additional theoretical and observational data were not yet available from which it has since been inferred that it is the earth which revolves round the sun. If, then, a belief may be rational and yet false, may not the religious man's belief be of this kind? May it not be that when the data of religious experience are supplemented in the believer's mind by further data provided by the sciences of psychology or sociology, it ceases to be rational for him to believe in God? Might it not then be rational for him instead to believe that his 'experience of the presence of God' is to be understood as an effect of a buried infancy memory of his father as a benevolent higher power; or of the pressure upon him of the human social organism of which he is a cell; or in accordance with some other naturalistic theory of the nature of religion?

Certainly this is possible. Indeed we must say, more generally, that all our beliefs, other than our acceptance of logically self-certifying propositions, are in principle open to revision or retraction in the light of new data. It is always conceivable that something which it is now rational for us to believe, it may one day not be rational for us to believe. But the difference which this general principle properly makes to our present believing varies from a maximum in relation to beliefs involving a considerable theoretical element, such as the higher-level hypotheses of the sciences, to a minimum in relation to perceptual beliefs, such as the belief that I now see a sheet of paper before me. And I have argued that so far as the great primary religious figures are concerned, belief in the reality of God is closer to the latter in that it is analogous to belief in the reality of the perceived material world. It is not an explanatory hypothesis, logically comparable with those developed in the sciences, but a perceptual belief. God was not, for Amos or Jeremiah or Jesus of Nazareth, an inferred entity but an experienced personal presence. If this is so, it is appropriate that the religious man's belief in the reality of God should be no more provisional than his belief in the reality of the physical world. The situation is in each case that, given the experience which he has and which is part of him, he cannot help accepting as 'there' such aspects of his environment as he experiences. He cannot help believing either in the reality of the material world which he is conscious of inhabiting, or of the personal divine presence which is overwhelmingly evident to him and to which his mode of living is a free response. And I have been suggesting that it is *as* reasonable for him to hold and to act upon the one belief as the other.

(d) The problem of conflicting religious beliefs

We must now take note of another circumstance which qualifies and threatens to erode our analogy. What are we to make of the immense variety of the forms of religious experience, giving rise as they do to apparently incompatible beliefs? In contrast to this, human sense experience reveals a world which is public in that normally the perceptions of any two individuals can readily be correlated in terms of the hypothesis of a common world which they jointly inhabit.

The variety commonly brought under the name of religion is indeed as wide as the range of man's cultural and psychological diversities. By no means all religious experience is theistic; ultimate reality is apprehended as non-personal and as multi-personal as well as unipersonal. And if we choose to extend the notion of religious experience, as Abraham Maslow has recently done by his concept of peak-experiences, (17) the variety is multiplied again. But even apart from this last expansion of the field it is clearly true that religious experience is bewilderingly varied in content and that the different reports to which it gives rise cannot easily be correlated as alternative accounts of the same reality. And therefore since one could restate the argument of the earlier part of this chapter from the point of view of many different religions, with their different forms of religious experience and belief, the question arises whether the argument does not prove too much. In establishing the rationality of the Judaic-Christian theist's belief in the reality of God, must it not also and equally establish the rationaltiy of the Buddhist's belief, arising out of *his* own coercive religious experience, and likewise of Hindu belief and of Islamic belief, and so on?

We need, I think, have no hesitation in accepting this implication. The principle which I have used to justify as rational the faith of a Christian who on the basis of his own religious experience cannot help believing in the reality of 'the God and Father of our Lord Jesus Christ', also operates to justify as rational the faith of a Muslim who on the basis of *his* religious experience cannot help believing in the reality of Allah and his providence; and the faith of the Buddhist who on the basis of *his* religious experience cannot help accepting the Buddhist picture of the universe; and so on.

But this is not the end of the matter. Various possibilities now open before us. I can only in conclusion attempt a small-scale map of the different paths that may be taken, showing in what direction they each lead and forecasting to some extent the kind of difficulties that are to be expected if one chooses to travel along them.

The first fork in the road is constituted by the alternative possibilities that the truth concerning the nature of the universe will, and that it will not, ultimately be a matter of public knowledge. The question is whether there will eventually be a situation in which all rational persons will find themselves obliged to agree, on the basis of a common body of experience, that the universe has this or that specific character. The issue, in other words, is that of the ultimate public verifiability and falsifiability of religious faiths.

On the one hand, in one conceivable picture of the universe it is possible for adherents of different and incompatible faiths to remain, so long as they continue to exist and to hold beliefs, under the impression that their own understanding of the universe is true; for they never meet an experiential crux which either verifies or falsifies their faith. This is a not always acknowledged feature of the pictures adopted both by the non-eschatological religions and by most atheistic and naturalistic theories. On the other hand, in another possible picture of the universe, or rather family of pictures painted by the different eschatological religions, the future development of human experience will narrow down the options until eventually only one faith is compatible with the facts and it becomes irrational to hold any contrary view. Thus it is affirmed in Christianity, in Islam, in one type of Judaism and perhaps in one type of Buddhism that the universe has a certain definite structure and is moving towards a certain definite fulfilment such that in the light of that fulfilment it will be beyond rational doubt that the universe has the particular character that it has.

Both types of universe are logically possible. If Christianity is true we are living in a universe of the latter type, in which religious faith is ultimately verified; and since we are now investigating the rationality of the Christian belief in God we shall want at this first fork to take the verifiability-of-faiths

118

option in order to explore it further and to see where it leads.

Travelling along this path, then, we now meet a second fork in the road, offering two rival conceptions of the relations between the different religions. Along one path we affirm the ultimate compatibility of the plurality of religious faiths, whilst along the other path we deny this. The latter, incompatibility thesis leads us to the following picture: it is at the moment rational for adherents of different religions, whose experience is such that they cannot help believing as they do, to hold their respective beliefs. But — still assuming the verifiability-of-faiths thesis — it will eventually cease to be possible for rational persons to adhere to rival and incompatible understandings of the universe. For according to this option in its strongest form, there is one true faith and many false ones — this view corresponding of course to the traditional dogmatic stances of the eschatological religions, such as Christianity and Islam. There is however a specifically Christian reason for abandoning this stance. This is that belief in the redeeming love of God for all his human creatures makes it incredible that the divine activity in relation to mankind should have been confined to those within the reach of the influence of the Christian revelation. The majority of the human beings who have existed since man began have lived either before or outside the historical influence of Jesus of Nazareth. Thus the doctrine that there is no salvation outside historic Christianity would in effect deny the universal love and redeeming activity of God.

Any modification of that traditional claim soon leads us over onto the alternative path, at the end of which lies the conclusion that the different forms of religious experience, giving rise to the different religions of the world, are properly to be understood as experiences of different aspects of one immensely complex and rich divine reality. If this is so, the beliefs of the different religions will be related to a larger truth as the experiences which gave rise to those beliefs are related to a larger reality.

The further exploration of this possibility would take us beyond our present necessarily limited inquiry. I have argued that when on the basis of his own compelling religious experience someone believes in the reality of God, he is believing rationally; and I have added the rider that when we

119

Notes

INTRODUCTION

1. For an account of this analysis see below, pp. 82-3.

2. 'Systematic Theology', I (Chicago: University of Chicago Press, 1951) p. 237; (London: Nisbet, 1953) pp. 262-3. Cf. John E. Smith, 'Experience and God' (New York and London: Oxford University Press, 1968) pp. 118-20.

3 'The Existence of God', Russell 'Why I am Not a Christian' (London: Allen & Unwin, 1957) p. 151.

4. Parts of my Introduction to 'The Existence of God' are reproduced, with the publishers' permission, in this Introduction and in Ch. 2 (c) and Ch. 7 (a).

CHAPTER 1

1. One could distinguish between a design argument with a basis restricted to the fact that the universe exhibits order, being a cosmos rather than a chaos, and one which goes beyond this to stress the teleological character of the evolution of the universe in producing man and the values of which he is conscious. I shall not however discuss these two varieties separately, since the strongest design arguments comprehend both considerations.

2. Plato, 'Laws', X.

3. Cicero, 'On the Nature of the Gods', II v, trans. C. D. Yonge (London: Bell, 1911) p. 50.

4. A series of lectures on Christian apologetics founded by a bequest from Robert Boyle (1627-91).

5. 'Philosophical Theology', II (Cambridge University Press, 1930).

6. 'Does God Exist?' (London: Macmillan, 1945).

7. 'Human Destiny' (London and New York: Longmans, Green, 1947).

8. 'Metaphysics' (Englewood Cliffs, N.J., and London: Prentice-Hall, 1963).

9. 'Natural Theology', ch. 1.

10. Whether Paley's point constitutes an adequate reply to Hume's will be considered presently, in note 25.

11. 'Natural Theology', Ch. 1.

12. Ibid.

13. 'Natural Theology', ch. 3.

14. Ibid.

15. William Derham, 'Physico-Theology', 9th ed. (London, 1737) pp. 257-8.

16. William Derham, 'Astro-Theology', 8th ed. (London, 1741) pp. 124-5.

17. Arthur I. Brown, 'Footprints of God' (Findlay, Ohio: Fundamental Truth Publishers, 1943) p. 102.

18. Cf. N. Kemp Smith, introduction to 'Hume's Dialogues concerning Natural Religion' (Oxford: Clarendon Press, 1935) app. C.

19. For a survey of theories about whom Cleanthes represents (for example Butler, or Berkeley), see Anders Jeffner, 'Butler and Hume on Religion' (Stockholm: Acta Universitatis Upsaliensis, Studia Doctrinae Christianae, No. 7, 1966) pp. 131 f.

20. Kemp Smith, p. 76. Hume's writings on religion are all in the same sceptical vein and style as that of Philo's speeches in the 'Dialogues'. Further, many of Philo's specific criticisms of the design argument occur in the 'Enquiry concerning the Human Understanding' (sect. XI). It is further evidence of Hume's desire to avoid direct formal responsibility for these criticisms, that here too he pretends to report them from a 'conversation with a friend who loves sceptical paradoxes'. (Humes' 'Enquiries', ed L. A. Selby-Bigge, 2nd ed. (Oxford: Clarendon Press, 1902) p. 132.) Burton F. Porter (in 'Deity and Morality' (London: Allen & Unwin, 1968) pp. 39-40) lists works in which Hume has been identified with Philo and Cleanthes respectively.

21. Pt II: Kemp Smith, p. 178.

22. Pt VII: Kemp Smith, p. 219.

23. Pt II: Kemp Smith, p. 183.

24. Pt IV: Kemp Smith, pp. 199-200. It is possible that Paley's fifth point (p. 4 above) was intended as a reply to this argument of Hume's — probably not however encountered in Hume's own writings (on this, see the next

note) but as used by someone else. But if so, no effective reply is made. For Hume was not suggesting that e.g. metal may form itself into watches by spontaneous motion, but rather that on the cosmic scale self-ordering may well be a property of matter. For we see in nature mind arising out of matter (since the human brain is formed within a biological process), as well as matter being ordered by mind.

25. Pt VIII: Kemp Smith, pp. 227-8. This is an argument against which Paley's fourth point (p. 4 above) may possibly have been directed. It would indeed be absurd, as Paley says, to suggest that since the matter composing a watch must take some form or other it is antecedently as likely to constitute a watch as anything else. But this is no answer to Hume's point, which is simply that any universe (as distinguished from a chaos) must be orderly and to that extent 'as though designed'. It therefore seems to me unlikely that Paley can have studied the 'Dialogues' for himself, although he may well have met elsewhere versions of some of Hume's arguments which had entered into the stream of public discussion. But this is conjecture; I know of no direct evidence.

26. Julian Huxley, 'The Evolutionary Process' in 'Evolution as a Process', ed. Julian Huxley, A. C. Hardy and E. B. Ford, 2nd ed. (London: Allen & Unwin, 1958) p. 4.

27. Ibid., p. 3. For a detailed account for the layman, see John Maynard Smith, 'The Theory of Evolution', 2nd ed. (Penguin Books, 1966).

28. 'An Enquiry Concerning Human Understanding', sect. XI: Selby-Bigge, p. 136. 'Dialogues', pt. V: Kemp Smith, p. 208.

29. Pt V: Kemp Smith, p. 207.

30. Pt V: Kemp Smith, p. 207.

31. Pt V: Kemp Smith, p. 209.

32. Pt II: Kemp Smith, p. 185.

33. Alvin Plantinga, 'God and Other Minds' (Ithaca, N.Y.: Cornell University Press, 1967) p. 101.

34. Cf. N. Kemp Smith, 'A Commentary to Kant's "Critique of Pure Reason"', 2nd ed. (London: Macmillan, 1923) p. 539, n. 3.

35. 'Human Destiny', p. 36.

36. Ibid., p. 202.

37. Ibid., p. 189.
38. Ibid., pp. 34-6.
39. Wallace I. Matson, 'The Existence of God' (Ithaca, N.Y.: Cornell University Press, 1965) pp. 102-11.
40. Ibid., p. 106.
41. Ibid., p. 107.
42. This research is described in A. O. Oparin, 'The Origin of Life on the Earth', trans Ann Synge, 3rd ed. (Edinburgh: Oliver & Boyd, 1957). See also J. Marquand, 'Life: Its Nature, Origins and Distribution' (Edinburgh: Oliver & Boyd, 1968).
43. Sidney Fox (Director of the Institute of Molecular Evolution, University of Miami), 'In the beginning . . . life assembled itself', 'New Scientist', 27 Feb 1969, p. 450.

CHAPTER 2

1. Though on the day on which this was written it was reported ('Guardian', 26 July 1968) that the Nederduits Gereformeerde Church, the largest of the three Dutch Reformed Churches in South Africa, has called for an immediate halt to the teaching of evolution in schools and universities!
2. 'Philosophical Theology', II 79.
3. Ibid., p. 81.
4. Ibid., p. 82.
5. Ibid., p. 83.
6. Ibid., p. 84.
7. Ibid., p. 85.
8. Ibid.
9. Ibid., p. 86.
10. Ibid., p. 87.
11. Ibid., p. 89.
12. Ibid., p. 93.
13. Ibid., p. 103.
14. Ibid., p. 113.
15. 'Metaphysics', p. 96.
16. Ibid., p. 96-7.
17. Ibid., p. 99.
18. Ibid., p. 100.

19. Ibid., pp. 100-1.

20. Ibid., p. 101.

21. Smith, 'The Theory of Evolution', p. 308.

22. For a slightly different criticism of Taylor's arguments, see Jan Narveson, 'On a new argument from design', 'Journal of Philosophy', LXII 9 (29 April 1965).

23. 'Philosophical Theology', II 245.

24. 'Theism', 'Encyclopaedia Britannica' (1962) XXII 50.

25. 'Towards Belief in God' (London S.C.M. Press, 1942) p. 112.

26. Cf. Arthur Pap, 'Elements of Analytic Philosophy' (New York: Macmillan, 1949) pp. 199-200.

27. 'Philosophical Theology', II 87.

28. Ibid., II 88.

29. Ibid., I 283.

30. 'Leviathan', pt 3, ch. 32.

31. 'Critique of Pure Reason', trans. Kemp Smith (London: Macmillan, and New York: St Martin's Press, 1933) p. 520.

32. Ibid.

CHAPTER 3

1. Leibniz, 'On the Ultimate Origination of Things', 'Philosophical Writings', ed. Mary Morris (London: Dent, and New York: Dutton, 1934) p. 32.

2. Aristotle, 'Physics', VII 1. Cf. 'Metaphysics', XII.

3. 'Summa Theologiae', ia 2, 3, trans. Timothy McDermott, O.P., new Dominican translation of the 'Summa Theologiae' (London: Eyre & Spottiswoode, and New York: McGraw-Hill, 1964) II 13-15.

4. These three kinds of *motus* were distinguished by Aristotle in 'Physics', V 226a.

5. Anthony Kenny, 'The Five Ways' (London: Routledge & Kegan Paul, 1969) ch. 2.

6. Ibid., p. 19.

7. Ibid., p. 21.

8. Ibid., p. 22.

9. Cf. 'Summa Theologiae', Ia, q. 46, art. 2; 'Summa contra Gentiles', II, chs 31-8.

10. A. D. Sertillanges, 'Sources de la Croyance en Dieu' (Paris: Perrin, 1905) pp. 64-72; R. Garrigou-Lagrange, 'God, His Existence and His Nature', trans. Dom Bede Rose (St Louis, Mo., and London: Herder, 1934-6) I 264 f.; E. L. Mascall, 'He Who Is: A Study in Traditional Theism' (London and New York: Longmans, Green 1943) ch. 5.

11. 'Summa Theologiae', I 15.

12. Cf. Kenny, 'The Five Ways', p. 40.

13. 'He Who Is', p. 46.

14. 'Aquinas' (Penguin Books, 1955) p. 118.

15. 'Aquinas', pp. 118-19.

16. 'Summa Theologiae', I 15.

17. In the version in the 'Summa Contra Gentiles' (I, ch. 15) Aquinas omits this stage of his argument.

18. Antony Flew, 'God and Philosophy' (London and New York: Hutchinson, 1966) pp. 101-2.

19. The principle of sufficient reason, 'in virtue of which we hold that there can be no fact real or existing, no statement true, unless there be a sufficient reason, why it should be so and not otherwise, although these reasons usually cannot be known to us': Leibniz, 'Monadology', 32.

20. Russell, 'Why I am not a Christian', p. 152.

21. Copleston, 'Aquinas', p. 124.

CHAPTER 4

1. 'Critique of Pure Reason', trans. Kemp Smith, p. 29.

2. 'Fundamental Principles of the Metaphysics of Morals', ch. 1, trans. H. J. Paton, 'The Moral Law' (London: Hutchinson, 1947) p. 61.

3. 'Critique of Practical Reason', trans. L. W. Beck (New York: Liberal Arts Press, 1956) p. 133.

4. Ibid., pp. 114-15.

5. Ibid., p. 119.

6. Ibid., p. 130.

7. Ibid., p. 130.

8. Ibid., p. 129.

9. Ibid., p. 133.

10. Ibid., p. 126.

11. 'The Theory of Good and Evil' (Oxford: Clarendon Press, 1907) II 208.

12. Ibid., II 212-13.

13. Rashdall adds in a footnote: 'Or at least a mind by which all Reality is controlled.'

14. Ibid., II 211-12.

15. 'A Grammar of Assent', ed. C. F. Harrold (New York and London: Longmans, Green, 1947) p. 83.

16. London: Allen & Unwin, 1954.

17. 'A Free Man's Worship', in 'Mysticism and Logic' (London: Longmans, Green, 1918) pp. 47-8. In 1962 Russell commented on this early essay that whilst he regarded its style as 'florid and rhetorical', nevertheless 'my outlook on the cosmos and on human life is substantially unchanged': 'Autobiography' (London: Allen & Unwin, 1969) III 172-3.

18. Margaret Knight, 'Morality — Supernatural or Social?', 'The Humanist Outlook', ed. A. J. Ayer (London: Pemberton, 1968) p. 47.

19. Of course if life has become a burden to him — if, for example, he is suffering the agony of a painful terminal illness — it may be rational for a man to abandon his life. But this is not the case that I am posing as a difficulty for humanist philosophy.

20. I owe this argument to Dr H. Stopes-Roe, and the counter to it to the Rev. Michael Goulder.

CHAPTER 5

1. 'Critique of Pure Reason', trans. Kemp Smith, p. 509.

2. Kant's argument about the dependence of the cosmological argument upon the ontological has been discussed, with differing results, by several philosophers: J. J. C. Smart, 'The Existence of God', in 'New Essays in Philosophical Theology', ed. Flew and MacIntyre (London: S.C.M. Press, and New York: Macmillan, 1955); T. Johnston, 'A Note on Kant's Criticism of the Arguments for the Existence of God', 'Australasian Journal of Philosophy', (1943); William H. Baumer, 'Kant on Cosmological Arguments', 'The Monist' (1967).

3. This name appears to have been given to the argument by Kant, the term 'ontology' having begun in the seventeenth century to be used to denote the 'science of being' and

having been popularised in the eighteenth century by Christian Wolff. By an ontological argument Kant apparently means an *a priori* argument leading to an existential conclusion.

4. It is clear from the references in Anselm's works that he had studied the writings of St Augustine both closely and extensively and accorded to them a very special authority. His high respect, almost veneration, for Augustine is expressed in the preface to the 'Monologion', where Anselm says: 'after frequent consideration, I have not been able to find that I have made in [the 'Monologion'] any statement which is inconsistent with the writings of the Catholic Fathers, or especially with those of St Augustine.' (Trans. S. N. Deane, 'St Anselm' (La Salle, Ill.: Open Court, 1958) p.36.)

5. 'On Free Will', II vi 14, trans. J. H. S. Burleigh in 'Augustine's Earlier Writings' (London: S.C.M. Press, and Philadelphia: Westminster Press, 1953) p. 144.

6. After long intellectual struggles, 'suddenly one night during matins the grace of God illuminated his heart, the whole matter became clear to his mind, and a great joy and exultation filled his inmost being.' ('Eadmer's Life of St Anselm', I, 19, trans. R. W. Southern (London: Nelson, 1962) p. 30.)

7. Augustine summarises his argument as follows: 'You admitted for your part that if I could show you something superior to our minds you would confess that it was God, provided nothing existed that was higher still. I accepted your admission and said it would be sufficient if I demonstrated that. If there is anything more excellent than wisdom, doubtless it, rather, is God. But if there is nothing more excellent, then truth itself is God. Whether there is or is not such a higher thing, you cannot deny that God exists, and this was the question set for our discussion.' ('On Free Will', II xv 39, Burleigh's trans., in 'Augustine's Earlier Writings', pp. 159-60.)

8. 'Pros.' 2. Within the same chapter he uses four variant forms: *aliquid quo maius nihil cogitari potest, id quo maius cogitari nequit, id quo maius cogitari non potest* and *aliquid quo maius cogitari non valet*. Elsewhere he uses yet other minor variations, such as *quo nil maius valet cogitari* ('Pros.'

128

5.) It is thus clear that no one precise form of words was essential to Anselm, and in discussing his argument I shall follow his example and use a variety of phrases.

9. Psalms 14:1 and 53:1.

10. Elsewhere he says, 'But I do not mean physically great, as a material object is great, but that which, the greater it is, is the better or more worthy.' ('Monologion', ch. 2.)

11. For example in 'Pros.' 14 and 18 Anselm uses the phrase *quo nihil melius cogitari potest*, and in various other places (e.g. 'Pros.' 3, 'Responsio', 8, 'Monol.' 4 and 15) he moves between *melius* and *maius*, or *bonum* and *magnum*, in a way which indicates their interchangeability within his argument.

12. 'Pros.' 15, Charlesworth's trans., 'St Anselm's Proslogion' (Clarendon Press, 1965) Cf. 'Responsio', 9 and 'Monol.' 64 and 65.

13. Karl Barth rightly insists upon the negative character of the formula. He says: 'All that the formula says about this object is, as far as I can see, this one thing, this one negative: nothing greater than it can be imagined; nothing can be imagined that in any respect whatsoever could or would outdo it; as soon as any conceives anything which in any respect whatsoever is greater than it, in so far as it can be conceived at all — then he has not yet begun to conceive it or has already ceased.' ('Anselm: Fides Quaerens Intellectum' (1931), trans. Ian W. Robertson (London: S.C.M. Press, 1960) p. 75.)

14. 'Pros.' 5 (Charlesworth's trans.).

15. There is a challenging discussion of this point in C. D. Broad, 'Religion, Philosophy and Psychical Research' (London: Routledge & Kegan Paul, 1953) pp. 177-80.

16. 'St Anselm's Proslogion', p. 57.

17. Leibniz's main contribution to the investigation of the ontological argument was to point out that it is an incomplete demonstration, 'which assumes something that must still be proved in order to render it mathematically evident; that is, it is tacitly assumed that this idea of the all-great or all-perfect being is possible, and implies no contradiction'. (Leibniz, 'New Essays Concerning Human Understanding', IV, ch. 10, trans. A. G. Langley (London: Macmillan, 1896) p. 504.) Leibniz himself held that 'We have

the right to presume the possibility of every being, and expecially that of God, until some one proves the contrary' (Ibid.), and that the onus lying upon the critic to demonstrate a contradiction in the concept of God has not been discharged. He accordingly concluded that 'according to the present state of our knowledge we must judge that God exists' (Ibid.). In appendix X he goes further and seeks to demonstrate the indemonstrability of the proposition, with regard to any two perfections, that they are incompatible.

18. 'Pros.' 2 (my italics): McGill's translation in 'The Many-faced Argument', ed. Hick and McGill (New York: Macmillan, 1967, and London: Macmillan, 1968).

19. 'Republic', 509.

20. It is a consequence of the equation of being with goodness than an absolutely evil being cannot exist, for to be absolutely devoid of goodness would be also to be absolutely devoid of being. It follows (as C. K. Grant pointed out in his 'The Ontological Disproof of the Devil', 'Analysis', XVII (Jan 1957) 71-2) that there cannot be an absolutely evil devil. The theologians who worked within the neoplatonist frame accepted this implcation, holding that the devil is good *qua* existent and *qua* powerful, etc., though wholly evil morally.

21. M. J. A. O'Connor 'New Aspects of Omnipotence and Necessity in Anselm', 'Religious Studies', IV (1968) 136.

22. Ibid.

23. 'The Many-faced Argument', ch. 3.

24. Gaunilo's 'Pro Insipiente', 6, trans. McGill in 'The Many-faced Argument', pp. 22-3.

25. 'Reply', 3, trans. McGill, ibid., p. 23.

26. 'Meditations', V, trans. Haldane and Ross, 'The Philosophical Works of Descartes', I (Cambridge, 1911) p. 182.

27. Ibid.

28. Ibid., I 180-1.

29. Ibid., I 181. The mountain and valley example is not a very good one, for there could be a mountain rising out of a plain, with no valley associated with it.

30. Ibid.

31. Ibid.

32. Ibid., II 186.

33. Ibid.

34. Ibid., II 228.

35. B 620-4 and B 625-30.

36. Kant's 'Critique of Pure Reason', trans. Kemp Smith, p. 502.

37. Ibid., p. 504.

38. Ibid., p. 505.

39. Ibid., pp. 504-5.

40. Bertrand Russell and A. N. Whitehead, 'Principia Mathematica', I (Cambridge, 1910) Introduction, ch. 1 and pt I,. sect. B, p. 14; Bertrand Russell, 'The Existential Import of Propositions', 'Mind' (1905) 398-401; 'On Denoting', 'Mind' (1905), reprinted in 'Readings in Philosophical Analysis', ed. Herbert Feigl and Wilfred Sellars, (New York: Appleton-Century Crofts, 1949); 'The Philosophy of Logical Atomism' (1918) V and VI, in 'Logic and Knowledge', ed. R. C. Marsh, (London: Allen & Unwin, 1956); 'Introduction to Mathematical Philosophy' (London: Allen & Unwin, 1920) ch. 16; 'History of Western Philosophy', (London: Allen & Unwin, 1946) pp. 859-60.

41. Cf. G. E. Moore, 'Is Existence a Predicate?' in 'Philosophical Papers' (London: Allen & Unwin, 1959) pp. 124-6.

42. Cf. P. Geach, 'Form and Existence' in 'Proceedings of the Aristotelian Society' (1954-5) 262-8. Reprinted in Geach, 'God and the Soul' (London: Routledge & Kegan Paul, 1969) pp. 54-60.

CHAPTER 6

1. E.g. J. N. Findlay, 'Can God's Existence be Disproved?', 'Mind' (April 1948), reprinted in 'New Essays in Philosophical Theology', ed. Flew and Macintyre, and elsewhere; J. J. C. Smart, 'The Existence of God' in 'New Essays in Philosophical Theology', pp. 38-9; and K. E. M. Baier, 'The Meaning of Life' (Canberra, 1957) p. 8. Although, I think, certainly mistaken, their idea is not absurd; for Avicenna had previously used a concept of logically necessary being, from which it seems that Aquinas was converted by Averroes' arguments by the time that he wrote the 'Summa contra Gentiles' and the 'Summa Theologiae'. (See Guy Jalbert, 'Nécessité et contingence chez S. Thomas D'Aquin et ses prédécesseurs' (Ottawa, 1961).)

2. Smart, in 'New Essays in Philosophical Theology' p. 40.

3. 'Responsio', 4: 'The Many-faced Argument', p. 28. Cf. 'Resp.' 1.

4. This paragraph embodies material from my article, 'Necessary Being', 'Scottish Journal of Theology' (Dec 1961). A closely related conception of necessary being has recently been related by Anthony Kenny to Aristotle's doctrine (in his 'De Interpretatione') that propositions are not timelessly true or false but may become true or cease to be true. Thus 'Theatetus is sitting' is true when Theatetus sits down but becomes false when he stands up. And since God is defined as an eternal being, without beginning or end, it follows that there is no time at which 'God exists' is false. Hence 'God exists' is a proposition which is true at all times and which is in this sense necessarily true. (Anthony Kenny, 'God and Necessity' in 'British Analytical Philosophy', ed. Bernard Williams and Alan Montefiore (London: Routledge & Kegan Paul, and New York: Humanities Press, 1966) pp. 147-51.) Cf. P. Æ. Hutchings, 'Necessary Being and Some Types of Tautology', 'Philosophy' (Jan 1964) 4-8; and Peter Geach in Anscombe and Geach, 'Three Philosophers' (Oxford: Blackwell, 1961) pp. 114-15, and 'God and the Soul', p. 77.

5. 'The Many-faced Argument', p. 355.

6. Cf. 'The Many-faced Argument', p. 356.

7. 'Recent Discussions of Anselm's Argument' in 'The Many-faced Argument', pp. 41-2.

8. 'Anselm: Fides Quaerens Intellectum', pp. 132 f.

9. 'Philosophical Review', LXIX (Jan 1960), reprinted in Malcolm's 'Knowledge and Certainty' (Englewood Cliffs, N.J.: Prentice-Hall, 1963) and elsewhere.

10. '[Anselm's] second proof employs the . . . principle that a thing is greater if it necessarily exists than if it does not necessarily exist. Some remarks about the notion of *dependence* may help to make this latter principle intelligible. Many things depend for their existence on other things and events. My house was built by a carpenter: its coming into existence was dependent on a certain creative activity. Its continued existence is dependent on many things: that a tree does not crush it, that it is not consumed by fire, and so on. If we reflect on the common meaning of

the word "God" . . . we realize that it is incompatible with this meaning that God's existence should *depend* on any-thing . . . . To conceive of anything as dependent upon something else for its existence is to conceive of it as a lesser being than God.' ('Knowledge and Certainty', pp. 146-7.)

11. 'Knowledge and Certainty', p. 149.

12. I am still using 'eternal' as short for 'eternal and independent'.

13. 'Knowledge and Certainty', p. 150.

14. Ibid., pp. 157-8.

15. 'Man's Vision of God' (Chicago, 1941; currently republished by Archon Books, Hamden, Conn.) 9; 'The Logic of Perfection' (La Salle, Ill.: Open Court, 1962) ch. 2; 'Anselm's Discovery' (La Salle, Ill. Open Court, 1965); 'The Formal Validity and Real Significance of the Ontological Argument', 'Philosophical Review' (1944); 'The Logic of the Ontological Argument', 'Journal of Philosophy', (1961); 'What did Anselm Discover?', 'Union Seminary Quarterly Review' (1962); and numerous smaller contributions.

16. Added at Hartshorne's request in the reprinting of this passage in 'The Many-faced Argument' (p. 335).

17. 'The Logic of Perfection', pp. 50-1.

18. Ibid., p. 53.

19. 'Responsio', 4: McGill, p. 28.

20. E.g. 'Of those who claim to demonstrate that the argument is a mere sophistry, the majority appear to have read the first page or so (Chapter II), or at least a paraphrase of it in some history, but one would be hard put to it in most cases to furnish evidence that they had read more.' ('Anselm's Discovery', p. 11. Cf. pp. 16-17.)

21. The redundant terms, in brackets, although odd, seem harmless.

22. 'Knowledge and Certainty', p. 150.

23. James F. Ross, 'Philosophical Theology' (New York: Bobbs-Merrill, 1969) p. 173.

24. Ibid., p. 174.

25. Ibid., p. 176.

CHAPTER 7

1. For a modern papal reaffirmation of the position that 'human reason can, without the help of divine revelation and grace, prove the existence of a personal God by arguments drawn from created things', see Pope Pius XII's encyclical 'Humani Generis' (1940), esp. paras 2, 3, 25 and 29.

2. See e.g. J. Oliver Buswell, 'What is God?' (Grand Rapids, Michigan: Zondervan, 1937), and Robert E. D. Clark, 'The Universe: Plan or Accident?' (Philadelphia: Muhlenberg Press, and London: Paternoster Press, 1961).

3. E.g. W. R. Matthews, 'Studies in Christian Philosophy', 2nd ed. (1928) and 'Theism' in 'Ency. Brit.' XXII 50.

4. See Abraham Heschel, 'God in Search of Man: A Philosophy of Judaism' (New York: Jewish Publication Society of America, 1955) pp. 246 f.; Martin Buber, 'Eclipse of God' (New York: Harper & Row, 1952, and London: Gonancy 1953) ch. 8.

5. E.g. John Baillie, 'Our Knowledge of God' (London: Oxford University Press, 1939) ch. 3, sect. 10.

6. 'Statement and Inference' (Oxford University Press, 1926) II 853.

7. 'God and Evil: a study of some relations between faith and morals', 'Ethics' (Jan 1958) 82.

8. 'Dialogues concerning Natural Religion', V.

9. 'Pensées', ed. Leon Brunschvicg, 430.

10. T. S. Eliot, 'Burnt Norton', I.

11. 'Metaphysical Beliefs' (London: S.C.M. Press, and New York: Allenson, 1957) p. 197. MacIntyre makes the same point in 'Difficulties in Christian Belief' (London: S.C.M. Press, 1960) p. 77.

12. J. H. Newman, 'A Grammar of Assent' (1870) ch. 4.

13. The exercise of this capacity is well described by C. S. Peirce as the unfolding of what he calls 'the humble argument' for the reality of God. See his 'Collected Papers' (Harvard University Press, 1934) 6.467 and 6.486.

14. This view is developed in my 'Faith and Knowledge', 2nd ed. (Ithaca, N.Y.: Cornell University Press, 1966, and London: Macmillan, 1967).

15. For a discussion of the notion of 'coerciveness' in sense experience and religious experience, see Donald F. Henze,

'Faith, Evidence, and Coercion', 'Philosophy' (Jan 1967) and John Hick, 'Faith and Coercion', 'Philosophy' (July 1967); and D. R. Duff-Forbes, 'Faith, Evidence, Coercion', 'Australasian Journal of Philosophy' (Aug 1969).

16. This is developed more fully in my 'Sceptics and Believers' in 'Faith and the Philosophers', ed. John Hick (London: Macmillan, and New York: St Martin's Press, 1964).

17. Abraham H. Maslow, 'Religions, Values, and Peak-Experiences' (Columbus, Ohio: Ohio State University Press, 1964).

Select Bibliography

(Works in foreign languages are listed under their English translations when such exist.)

WRITINGS DISCUSSING TWO OR MORE OF THE ARGUMENTS

Textbook expositions and discussions

H. J. Paton, 'The Modern Predicament' (London: Allen & Unwin, and New York: Macmillan, 1955).

Geddes MacGregor, 'Introduction to Religious Philosophy' (Boston, Mass.: Houghton Mifflin, and London: Macmillan, 1959).

John Hick, 'Philosophy of Religion' (Englewood Cliffs, N.J., and London: Prentice-Hall, 1963).

H. D. Lewis, 'Philosophy of Religion' (London: English Universities Press, and New York: Barnes & Noble, 1965).

Thomas McPherson, 'The Philosophy of Religion' (New York: Van Nostrand, 1965).

Frederick Ferré, 'Basic Modern Philosophy of Religion' (New York: Scribner's, 1967, and London; Allen & Unwin, 1968).

J. Hospers, 'An Introduction to Philosophical Analysis' 2nd ed. (Englewood Cliffs, N.J.: Prentice-Hall, and London: Routledge & Kegan Paul, 1967) ch. 5.

Works advocating some of the arguments

A. E. Taylor, 'Theism', 'Encyclopedia of Religion and Ethics', ed. Hastings, xii (Edinburgh, 1921, and New York: Scribner's, 1951).

——, 'Does God Exist?' (London and New York: Macmillan, 1945).

John Laird, 'Theism and Cosmology' (London: Allen & Unwin, 1941).

——, 'Mind and Deity' (London: Allen & Unwin, 1941).

G. H. Joyce, 'The Principles of Natural Theology' (London and New York: Longmans, Green, 1951).

Richard Taylor, 'Metaphysics' (Englewood Cliffs, N.J., and

London: Prentice-Hall, 1963) ch. 7.

A. C. Ewing, 'Two "Proofs" of God's Existence', 'Religious Studies' (1965).

James F. Ross, 'Philosophical Theology' (New York: Bobbs-Merrill, 1969).

Criticisms of the arguments

J. S. Mill, 'Three Essays on Religion' (London: Longmans, Green, 1874).

C. D. Broad, 'Arguments for the Existence of God', i and ii, 'Journal of Theological Studies' (1939), reprinted in 'Religion, Philosophy and Psychical Research' (London: Routledge & Kegan Paul, and New York: Harcourt, 1953).

J. J. C. Smart, 'The Existence of God', 'New Essays in Philosophical Theology', ed. Flew and MacIntyre (London: S.C.M. Press, and New York: Macmillan, 1955).

Bertrand Russell and F. C. Copleston, 'The Existence of God — a debate', in Russell, 'Why I am not a Christian' (London: Allen & Unwin, 1957). (Not included in U.S. edition.)

Walter Kaufmann, 'Critique of Religion and Philosophy' (New York: Harper, 1958, and London: Faber & Faber, 1959).

Wallace I. Matson, 'The Existence of God' (Ithaca, N.Y.: Cornell U.P., 1965).

Antony Flew, 'God and Philosophy' (London and New York: Hutchison, 1966).

Alvin Plantinga, 'God and Other Minds' (Ithaca, N.Y.: Cornell U.P., 1967).

THE DESIGN ARGUMENT

Works defending some form of design argument

William Paley, 'Natural Theology' (1802), abridged ed. by F. Ferré (Indianapolis: Bobbs-Merrill, 1963).

F. R. Tennant, 'Philosophical Theology' ii (Cambridge and New York: Cambridge U.P., 1930) ch. 4.

A. E. Taylor, 'Does God Exist?' (London and New York:

Macmillan, 1945).

Lecomte du Noüy, 'Human Destiny' (New York: Longmans, Green, 1947).

Peter Bertocci, 'Introduction to the Philosophy of Religion' (Englewood Cliffs, N.J.: Prentice-Hall, 1951) ch. 11-15.

Robert E. D. Clark, 'The Universe: Plan or Accident?' (Philadelphia: Muhlenberg Press, and London: Paternoster Press, 1961).

Richard Taylor, 'Metaphysics' (Englewood Cliffs, N.J., and London: Prentice-Hall, 1963) ch. 7.

Works criticising the design argument

David Hume, 'Dialogues concerning Natural Religion' (1779), critical ed. by N. Kemp Smith, 2nd ed. (Edinburgh and New York: Nelson, 1947).

Clarence Darrow, 'The Story of My Life' (New York: Scribner's, 1932) ch. 44.

Wallace I. Matson, 'The Existence of God' (Ithaca, N.Y.: Cornell U.P., 1965).

Discussions of various aspects

D. L. Scudder, 'Tennant's Philosophical Theology' (New Haven, Conn.: Yale U.P., and London: Oxford U.P., 1940).

Antony Flew, 'Hume's Philosophy of Belief' (London: Routledge & Kegan Paul, and New York: Humanities Press, 1961) ch. 9.

Anders Jeffner, 'Butler and Hume on Religion' (Stockholm: Diakonistyrelsens Bokförlag, 1966).

J. Marquand, 'Life: Its Nature, Origins and Distribution' (Edinburgh: Oliver & Boyd, and New York: W. A. Benjamin, 1968).

Norman Goldhawk, 'William Paley: or the Eighteenth Century Revisited', *Providence*, ed. Maurice Wiles (London: S.P.C.K., 1969).

Works defending the cosmological argument

Thomas Aquinas, 'Summa Theologiae', pt i, Q. 2, art. 3.
R. Garrigou-Lagrange, 'God, His Existence and His Nature', trans. Bede Rose, 2 vols (St Louis, Mo., and London: Herder, 1934-6).
R. P. Phillips, 'Modern Thomistic Philosophy', ii (Westminster Md: Newman Press, 1935).
Austin Farrer, 'Finite and Infinite' (London: Dacre, 1943, 2nd ed. 1959, and Naperville, Ill.: Allenson, 2nd ed., 1964).
E. L. Mascall, 'He Who Is' (London and New York: Longmans, Green, 1948).
Fernand Van Steenberghen, 'Ontology', trans. M. J. Flynn (New York: Wagner, and London: Herder, 1952).
Dom Illtyd Trethowan, 'An Essay in Christian Philosophy' (London and New York: Longmans, Green, 1954).
Samuel M. Thompson, 'A Modern Philosophy of Religion' (Chicago: Henry Regnery, 1955) pt 6.
Victor Preller, 'Divine Science and the Science of God: A Reformulation of Thomas Aquinas' (Princeton: Princeton U.P., 1967).

Works criticising the cosmological argument

David Hume, 'Dialogues Concerning Natural Religion' (1779) pt 9.
Paul Edwards, 'The Cosmological Argument', 'The Rationalist Annual' (1959).
W. E. Kennick, 'A New Way with the Five ways', 'Australasian Journal of Philosophy' (1960).
Anthony Kenny, 'The Five Ways' (London: Routledge & Kegan Paul, and New York: Schocken, 1969).

Discussions of various aspects

Ronald Hepburn, 'From World to God'. 'Mind' (1963).
——, 'Cosmological Arguments for the Existence of God', 'The Encyclopedia of Philosophy', ii (New York, 1967).

William H. Baumer, 'Kant on Cosmological Arguments', 'The Monist' (1967).

Ninian Smart, 'Philosophers and Religious Truth', 2nd ed. (London: S.C.M. Press, 1969) ch. 4.

Michael Durrant, 'St Thomas' "Third Way" ', 'Religious Studies' (1969).

MORAL ARGUMENTS

Works advocating some form of moral argument

Immanuel Kant, 'Critique of Practical Reason' (1788) ii, ch. 2, trans. L. W. Beck (New York: Liberal Arts Press, 1956).

John Henry Newman, 'A Grammar of Assent' (1870).

Hastings Rashdall, 'The Theory of Good and Evil' (Oxford U.P., 1907).

——, 'Philosophy and Religion' (London: Duckworth, 1909).

——, 'God and Man' (Oxford U.P., 1930).

W. R. Sorley, 'Moral Values and the Idea of God' (Cambridge U.P., 1918).

C. C. J. Webb, 'Divine Personality and Human Life' (London: Allen & Unwin, 1920).

D. M. Baillie, 'Faith in God' (Edinburgh: T. & T. Clark, 1927, and New York: Hillary, 1964) ch. 5.

John Baillie, 'The Interpretation of Religion' pt ii, chs 5-7 (Edinburgh: T. & T. Clark, 1929, and Nashville, Tenn.: Abingdon, 1965).

A. E. Taylor, 'The Faith of a Moralist' (London: Macmillan, 1930).

W. G. de Burgh, 'From Morality to Religion' (London: Macdonald & Evans, 1938).

Austin Farrer, 'A Starting-point for the Philosophical Examination of Theological Belief', 'Faith and Logic', ed. Basil Mitchell (London: Allen & Unwin, 1957, and New York: Humanities, 1958).

H. P. Owen, 'The Moral Argument for Christian Theism' (London: Allen & Unwin, 1965).

Works criticising moral arguments

C. A. Campbell, 'Selfhood and Godhood' (London: Allen & Unwin, and New York: Humanities, 1957).
140

W. G. Maclagan, 'The Theological Frontier of Ethics' (London: Allen & Unwin, and New York: Humanities, 1961).

Ronald Hepburn, 'Moral Arguments for the Existence of God', 'The Encyclopedia of Philosophy', v (New York, 1967).

Margaret Knight, 'Morality — Supernatural or Social?', 'The Humanist Outlook', ed. A. J. Ayer (London: Pemberton, 1968).

Discussions of various aspects

S. Körner, 'Kant' (London: Penguin, 1955) ch. 7.

H. J. Paton, 'The Modern Predicament' (London: Allen & Unwin, and New York: Macmillan, 1955) ch. 21.

John R. Silber, 'Kant's Conception of the Highest Good as Immanent and Transcendent', 'The Philosophical Review' (1959).

A. C. Ewing, 'The Autonomy of Ethics', 'Prospect for Metaphysics', ed. Ian Ramsey (London: Allen & Unwin, and New York: Philosophical Library, 1961).

D. A. Rees, 'Metaphysical Schemes and Moral Principles', 'Prospect for Metaphysics', ed. Ian Ramsey.

Burton F. Porter, 'Deity and Morality' (London: Allen & Unwin, and New York: Humanities, 1968).

THE ONTOLOGICAL ARGUMENT

Classical treatments

Anselm, 'Proslogion', chs 2-4, 'Reply' by Gaunilo, and 'Response' by Anselm: Latin and English on facing pages, ed. and trans. M. J. Charlesworth (Oxford U.P., 1965).

Descartes, 'Meditations', v, and 'Objections' i, ii and v with Descartes' 'Replies', trans. Haldane and Ross, 'The Philosophical Works of Descartes', ii (Cambridge U.P., 1912, and New York: Dover, 1934).

Spinoza, 'Ethics', pt i, props 7-11, trans. R. H. M. Elwes (London: Bohn's Philosophical Library, 1883-4).

Leibniz, 'New Essays Concerning Human Understanding', iv, ch. 10 and app. x, trans. A. G. Langley (London and New

York: Macmillan, 1896); 'Monadology', sects 44-5, trans.
R. Latta (Oxford U.P., 1898).

Kant, Critique of Pure Reason: Transcendental Dialectic', ii,
ch. iii, sect. 4, trans. N. Kemp Smith (London: Macmillan,
and New York: St Martin's Press, 1933).

Hegel, 'Lectures on the Philosophy of Religion', appendix,
trans. E. B. Speirs and J. B. Sanderson (London: Kegan
Paul, 1895).

Historical

C. C. J. Webb, 'Anselm's Ontological Argument for the
Existence of God', 'Proceedings of the Aristotelian
Society' (1896).

R. Miller, 'The Ontological Argument in Anselm and
Descartes', 'The Modern Schoolman' (1954-5 and 1955-6).

'Spicilegium Beccense', Proceedings of the Congrés International du IXe Centenaire de l'arrivée d'Anselme au Bec
(Paris: Vrin, 1959).

Deiter Henrich, 'Der ontologische Gottesbeweis: sein
Problem und seine Geschichte in der Neuzeit' (Tübingen:
J. C. B. Mohr, 2nd ed., 1967).

S. M. Engel, 'Kant's "Refutation" of the Ontological
Argument', 'Philosophy and Phenomenological Research'
(1963).

Alvin Plantinga, 'Kant's Objection to the Ontological
Argument', 'Journal of Philosophy' (1966).

A. C. McGill, 'Recent Discussions of Anselm's Argument',
'The Many-faced Argument: Recent studies on the
Ontological Argument for the Existence of God', ed. John
Hick and A. C. McGill (New York: Macmillan, 1967, and
London: Macmillan, 1968).

Important varying interpretations

Étienne Gilson, 'Sens et nature de l'argument de Saint
Anselm', 'Archives d'histoire doctrinale et littéraire du
moyen age' (1934).

142

Anselm Stolz, 'Anselm's Theology in the Proslogion', trans. A. C. McGill, 'The Many-faced Argument'.

Karl Barth, 'Anselm: Fides Quaerens Intellectum', trans. Ian Robertson (London: S.C.M. Press, and New York: Meridian, 1960).

The Hegelian use of the argument

Edward Caird, 'Anselm's Argument for the Being of God', 'Journal of Theological Studies' (1899).

W. E. Hocking, 'On the Ontological Argument in Royce and Others', 'Contemporary Idealism in America', ed. C. Barrett (New York: Macmillan, 1932).

R. G. Collingwood, 'Philosophical Method' (Oxford U.P., 1933) ch. 6.

Gilbert Ryle, 'Mr Collingwood and the Ontological Argument', 'Mind' (1935); 'Back to the Ontological Argument', 'Mind' (1937).

E. E. Harris, 'Mr Ryle and the Ontological Argument', 'Mind' (1936).

Aimé Forest, 'St Anselm's Argument in Reflexive Philosophy', trans. A. C. McGill, 'The Many-faced Argument'.

The second form of the argument

Charles Hartshorne, 'Man's Vision of God' (New York: Harper, 1941).

——, 'The Logic of Perfection' (La Salle, Ill.: Open Court, 1962).

——, 'Anselm's Discovery' (La Salle, Ill.: Open Court, 1965).

——, 'The Formal Validity and Real Significance of the Ontological Argument', 'Philosophical Review' (1944).

——, 'The Logic of the Ontological Argument', 'Journal of Philosophy' (1961).

——, 'What Did Anselm Discover?', 'Union Seminary Quarterly Review' (1962).

J. O. Nelson, 'Modal Logic and the Ontological Proof for God's Existence', 'Review of Metaphysics' (1963).

J. B. Cobb, ' "Perfection Exists": A Critique of Charles Hartshorne', 'Religion in Life' (1963).

Julian Hartt, 'The Logic of Perfection', 'Review of Metaphysics' (1963).

David Pailin, 'Some Comments on Hartshorne's Presentation of the Ontological Argument', 'Religious Studies' (1968).

Norman Malcolm, 'Anselm's Ontological Arguments', 'Philosophical Review' (1960), reprinted in 'Knowledge and Certainty', (Englewood Cliffs, N.J.: Prentice-Hall, 1963). Discussion by R. E. Allen, R. Abelson, T. Penelhum, A. Plantinga, P. Henle and G. B. Matthews, 'Philosophical Review' (1961).

T. P. Brown, 'Professor Malcolm on "Anselm's Ontological Arguments" ', 'Analysis' (1961).

John Hick, 'A Critique of the "Second Argument" ', 'The Many-faced Argument'.

Other important modern discussions

J. N. Findlay, 'Can God's Existence be Disproved?', 'Mind' (1948), reprinted in 'New Essays in Philosophical Theology', ed. Flew and MacIntyre (London: S.C.M. Press, and New York: Macmillan, 1955).

Robert J. Richman, 'The Ontological Proof of the Devil', 'Philosophical Studies' (1958).

Nicholas Rescher, 'The Ontological Proof Revisited', 'Australasian Journal of Philosophy' (1959).

William Alston, 'The Ontological Argument Revisited', 'Philosophical Review' (1960).

J. Schaffer, 'Existence, Predication and the Ontological Argument', 'Mind' (1962), reprinted in 'The Many-faced Argument'.

Alvin Plantinga, 'God and Other Minds' (Ithca, N.Y.: Cornell U.P., 1967) chs 1-3.

M. J. A. O'Connor, 'New Aspects of Omnipotence and Necessity in Anselm', 'Religious Studies' (1968).

Charles Crittenden, 'The Argument from Perfection to Existence', 'Religious Studies' (1968).

THE IDEA OF NECESSARY BEING IN THE ONTOLOGICAL AND COSMOLOGICAL ARGUMENTS

A. N. Prior, 'Is Necessary Existence Possible?', 'Philosophy and Phenomenological Research' (1955). R. L. Franklin, 'Necessary Being', 'Australasian Journal of Philosophy' (1957).

P. Æ. Hutchings, 'Necessary Being', 'Australasian Journal of Philosophy' (1957).

——, 'Necessary Being and Some Types of Tautology', 'Philosophy' (1964).

Richard Robinson, 'Necessary Propositions', 'Mind' (1958).

John Hick, 'God as Necessary Being', 'Journal of Philosophy' (1960).

——, 'Necessary Being', 'Scottish Journal of Theology' (1961).

T. Penelhum, 'Divine Necessity', 'Mind' (1960).

W. E. Abraham, 'Is the Concept of Necessary Existence Self Contradictory?', 'Inquiry' (1962).

J. F. Ross, 'God and Logical Necessity', 'Philosophical Quarterly' (1961).

Guy Jalbert, 'Necessité et Contingence chez saint Thomas d'Aquin et chez ses Prédecesseurs' (Ottawa: Editions de l'Université d'Ottawa, 1961).

Anthony Kenny, 'Necessary Being', 'Sophia' (1962).

——, 'God and Necessity', 'British Analytical Philosophy', ed. Bernard Williams and Alan Montefiore (London: Routledge & Kegan Paul, and New York: Humanities Press, 1966).

R. Puccetti, 'The Concept of God', 'Philosophical Quarterly' (1964).

Patterson Brown, 'St Thomas' Doctrine of Necessary Being', 'Philosophical Review' (1964).

J. N. Findlay, 'Some Reflections on Necessary Existence', 'Process and Divinity', ed. William Reese and Eugene Freeman (La Salle, Ill.: Open Court, 1964).

Alvin Plantinga, 'Necessary Being', 'Faith and Philosophy', ed. Plantinga (Grand Rapids, Michigan: Eerdman, 1964).

John Baillie, 'Our Knowledge of God' (London: Oxford U.P., and New York: Scribner's, 1939).

——, 'The Sense of the Presence of God' (London: Oxford U.P., and New York: Scribner's, 1962).

H. Richard Niebuhr, 'The Meaning of Revelation' (New York: Macmillan, 1941).

Erich Frank, 'Philosophical Understanding and Religious Truth' (London and New York: O.U.P., 1945). ·

John Hick, 'Faith and Knowledge' (1957), 2nd ed. (Ithaca, N.Y.: Cornell U.P., 1966, and London: Macmillan, 1967).

H. D. Lewis, 'Our Experience of God' (London: Allen & Unwin, and New York: Macmillan, 1959).

Austin Farrer, 'Faith and Speculation' (London: Black, and New York: New York U.P., 1967).

Alvin Plantinga, 'God and Other Minds' (Ithaca, N.Y.: Cornell U.P., 1967).

Diogenes Allen, 'The Reasonableness of Faith' (Cleveland, Ohio: Corpus Books, 1968).

Index

McGill, A. C., 76, 90
MacIntyre, Alasdair, 105
Malcolm, Norman, 70, 91 f.
Marquand, J., 124
Mascall, E. L., 43
Maslow, Abraham, 117
Matson, Wallace I., 16 f.
Matthews, W. R., 27, 134
Moore, G. E., 131
Moral arguments, 53 f.
Morality, 20-1, 31, 53 f.
Motion, argument from, 38 f.
Mystery, 34 f.

Narveson, Jan, 125
Natural belief, 47, 110
Necessary being, 46, 84 f., 103, 132-3
Neoplatonism, 71, 73
Newman, J. H., 58-59, 106, 107

O'Connor, M. J., 74 f.
Ontological argument, ix, 68 f., 104; 'first form', 70 f.; 'second form', 84 f.
Oparin, A. O., 124

Paley, William, 2, 3 f., 14, 18, 122, 123
Paley's Watch, 3 f.
Pascal, B., 104
Peirce, C. S., 134
Plantinga, Alvin, 13-14
Plato, vii, 1, 73
Pope Pius XII, 134
Porter, Burton F., 122
Prime mover, 38 f.

Probability, xii, 13-14, 27 f., 101; alogical, 29 f.
Proof, ix f.
Protestantism, 101

Rashdall, Hastings, 57 f., 127
Rationality, 108 f.
Ray, John, 3
Religious experience, 109 f., 111 f., 117 f.
Roman Catholicism, 101
Ross, James F., 97 f.
Russell, Bertrand, viii, xi, 51, 58, 60 f., 82-3, 85, 131

Sartre, J.-P., 51
Sertillanges, A. D., 126
Smart, J. J. C., 85-6, 127
Smith, John E., 121
Smith, J. M., 123, 125
Smith, N. Kemp, 8
Solipsism, 110, 112-113
Stoics, vii
Stopes-Roe, H. V., 127
Sufficient reason, principle of, 37, 43

Taylor, A. E., 2
Taylor, Richard, 2, 21 f.
Teleological argument, see Design argument
Tennant, F. R., 2, 14, 18 f., 27, 28-9
Tillich, Paul, viii

Whitehead, A. N., 131
Wilson, J. Cook, 102-3
Wolff, C., 53. 128

148